EMOTIONALLY DISTURBED CHILDREN

CONTRIBUTORS

Peter Knoblock/Syracuse University/editor

William M. Cruickshank/Syracuse University

Louis M. Smith/Washington University

William C. Morse/University of Michigan

William C. Rhodes/Peabody College

Harry Krohn/Hawthorne Cedar Knolls School

Edward J. Murray/Syracuse University

Rosalyn S. Cohen/Children's Day Treatment Center and School

Ruth Lavietes/Children's Day Treatment Center and School

Renee Reens/Children's Day Treatment Center and School

Bianca Rindsberg/Children's Day Treatment Center and School

EDUCATIONAL PROGRAMMING
for
EMOTIONALLY DISTURBED CHILDREN:

THE DECADE AHEAD

PETER KNOBLOCK, Ph.D., *Editor*

Division of Special Education and Rehabilitation
Syracuse University

Proceedings of The First Annual Conference
on the Education of Emotionally Disturbed Children

This publication made possible through
Syracuse University Division of Special Education and Rehabilitation

For additional copies write to
Division of Special Education and Rehabilitation
805 South Crouse Avenue
Syracuse, New York 13210

price $2.50

MANUFACTURED IN THE UNITED STATES OF AMERICA
BY THE PRINTING DIVISION, SYRACUSE UNIVERSITY PRESS

TABLE OF CONTENTS

FOREWORD

Some phase of education is continually at a crossroads stage. As this collection of papers is published, public schools and public school educators are at such a point with reference to emotionally disturbed children.

Three decades ago public schools were little concerned with the ongoing program for emotionally disturbed children. True, educators as humanitarians were thoughtfully aware of these children. Educators were often perplexed as to the behavior of emotionally disturbed children and for their future. However, there was no major proponent for the argument that this was a basic problem of the public schools. Indeed, there were strong points of view being held by representatives of non-educational groups which argued that this was not a problem of the public schools. Advocates of the mental health movement of the time urged the establishment of child guidance centers, mental health clinics, and diagnostic and treatment programs to which the schools, along with other agencies or individuals, could refer children with emotional problems. These centers and clinics were to be placed under the direction of psychiatric personnel. Concepts of treatment and therapy were in no way a part of the philosophy of most public school administrators, who were thus quite willing to either avoid the assumption of a non-educational problem or to call their work done in the support of mental health clinics in the community.

As important as this movement was and is, the problem of the emotionally disturbed child in American life has not been solved by its efforts. The mental health movement of the thirties and forties, while accomplishing much, fell short of its goals and the hopes for it. Lack of sufficient psychological, psychiatric, and other types of personnel has meant that sufficient treatment centers have never been developed. Those which have been put into operation have never been able to avoid a long waiting list nor have they generally received other than emergency problems. The lack of qualified personnel has been accentuated since 1945 by the increase in the child population and by the increase in the number of children needing services. These two opposing trends have italicized a problem as severe and pressing to which the nation can not further avoid recognition.

1

The public schools in their enviable position of acceptance by the community, with their reputation for interest in children, with their willingness to experiment, and with a long history of accepting responsibility for exceptional children of many different types have, in the face of the limited community mental health programs, obviously been the agency to which the community leaders have now turned for help in the solution of the problem. Public school boards of education, administrators and teachers have often made genuine efforts to respond to this community request, usually without adequate information, training, or support. In some school systems good services have been extended to disturbed children. However, the wave of concern which is currently observable in the United States and Canada demands an educational thrust which goes far beyond the programs which are in operation. The demands for quality programs and the genuine needs on which such demands are based further underscores the problems which are faced.

Teachers must be prepared and these must be prepared with a depth of understanding not typical of teacher education programs of the past. Administrative attitudes toward these programs must be modified to make them welcome in the public schools. The public schools' responsibility for treatment and therapy *versus* educational programs based on normal expectancies must be analyzed and accepted. The role of non-educational personnel in the public school setting must be worked through by the professions involved and the changing roles of some professions must be understood and accepted by them. The fiscal support of long-term programs which often produce small dividends must be thoroughly understood and supported by the communities. These and a myriad of other significant problems will need administrative and community insights before the challenge of the emotionally disturbed child can adequately be met. Time, however, is limited. Without these matters being solved and accepted as working principles in a community, the public school programs will never be more conclusive than the mental health movement has been, and the needs are many-fold greater today than thirty years past.

Public educators, college and university personnel, and personnel of community agencies related to the education of emotionally disturbed children face the challenge of basing this educational thrust on something more than methods-and-materials courses which have so long typified American teacher education. This approach cannot meet the challenge which is presently facing thoughtful educators. A new look, undercutting many things which have thus far been tried must be the goal which is to be achieved.

The collection of papers which is included herein aims to create new activity at the cutting edge. Through a new look at research methodology as suggested by Dr. Louis M. Smith, through a new evaluation of intervention techniques proposed by Dr. William Morse, and by a new perspective applied to community action suggested by Dr. William Rhodes, the problem of educating emotionally disturbed children in the broadest sense begins to come into a different and perhaps new focus. Research, intervention techniques, community action, and education *per se* as underscored by Mr. Harry Krohn and others, in concert become the vehicles through which a public educational program may become effective in meeting the needs of emotionally disturbed children.

The education of emotionally disturbed children and the inclusion of such programs in public educational services is not merely a matter of administrative decision. Vital programs involve much more. The long-term effectiveness of this important phase of education will be insured only when the ideas nested in the significant papers which follow — along with others — are translated into dynamic action-research, and when sustained educational activities for emotionally disturbed children are couched in a vital philosophy, realistic administrative understanding, creative teaching based on psychological principles, and extensive community support of the highest order of finance and understanding.

WILLIAM M. CRUICKSHANK

Syracuse, New York

1965

3

PREFACE

This Conference, like the field of educating emotionally disturbed children, developed slowly and then gained momentum. In many other ways, the development and implementation of the Conference closely parallels the broad field with which the sessions concerned themselves. For example, we were confronted with definitional problems as to the type of child we should be discussing; deciding which professional groups had spheres of interest in educational programming; and perhaps most importantly the ever-present problem of clearly articulating our goal. As Dr. Morse indicates in his summary discussion it behooves us to operate on several levels simultaneously. Namely, while we are occupying ourselves with the immediate program needs of these children it is as necessary to develop long-range goals and programming approaches.

Those of us engaged in the designing of this Conference approached the task with great conviction as well as with great trepidation. Despite our awareness of the growing interest in the education of disturbed children we were uncertain as to what professional groups would be attracted to such a series of meetings. Thus we were confronted with one of the issues prominent in the field — namely to which professional workers do we turn for leadership and direction? Or, are the educational and emotional problems presented by these children of such magnitude that many types of school practitioners find themselves actively focusing on their needs? While we must await a definitive answer to this question, a detailed analysis of those attending this Conference supports the latter belief. While a large number attending were practitioners already functioning in school and clinical settings with disturbed children, a great many others were engaged in regular school programs as teachers, administrators, or were training for elementary education positions.

This wide range of interests is one observation we have had forcefully pointed out to us in many ways. Attendance at workshops, convention meetings, and other organized gatherings which deal with education of disturbed children is invariably heavy as are University courses in this area when enrollment is made available to public school personnel. In the near future, those of us involved in the preparation of personnel must conceptualize meaningful ways to not only capture such interest but sustain it on the part of many diverse professional workers. Confronted with this high interest level plus the staggering numbers of disturbed children in need of programming it would seem imperative for us to broaden the base of our training patterns to include not only preparation of specialized personnel but the sensitizing and training of many other groups already actively engaged with disturbed children, such as school nurses, elementary and secondary school teachers and administrators, and pupil personnel workers.

Almost immediately, we were confronted with a number of strategic planning questions. There was the question of a Conference theme. Do we attempt to deal with a specific or reasonably well-circumscribed topic or should the coverage be somewhat broader? Behind this rested a more crucial issue confronting our field. Namely, do we need to analyze what has gone on in the past and in related special education fields in order to chart our course? Or is it more advantageous for us to carefully interpret and re-interpret our current practices with an eye toward modification and implementation of new practices? A dramatic example of the former approach is the current investment in interest and funding directed toward the development of special classes for emotionally disturbed children. This particular intervention program is one which is modeled closely after classes for mentally retarded and physically handicapped children. The uncritical acceptance of such an approach has resulted in many communities placing great hope in the efficacy of such programs without a sound understanding of the conditions contributing to its success or failure. An evaluation of what transpired at this Conference would indicate that the speakers and participants generally straddled this issue leaning first in one direction and then in another. It would seem as if workers faced with the dilemma of not being completely satisfied with what they are doing in terms of programming for disturbed children keep looking for chinks in the armor when perhaps they should create great upheavals in their thinking and approaches.

It is well recognized by those actively engaged in programs for disturbed children that we have carved out a field of study that cuts across many disciplines. With this in mind, the speakers as well as those attending, represented several professional groups and points of view. If one can pinpoint a "feeling," it might be accurate to say that the speakers all seemed to fit into our model of the "worker with disturbed children," despite the fact that they did represent several disciplines. In a time of great uncertainty and hesitancy on the part of legislatures, state education departments and school administrators to design programs for disturbed children, it is significant that approximately 600 to 800 individuals attended this Conference without wilting under the kinds of ambiguities that have served to immobilize large groups of professionals when we have asked them to address their attention to the educational needs of disturbed children. There was a kind of intensity and keenness of interest demonstrated by those attending which enabled the speakers to focus on creative juxtaposing of past and present concepts in an effort to reformulate and plan ahead. Similarly, the spontaneous reaction of a great many who attended clearly indicated a continuance of this Conference in future years. It would seem that many messages were being conveyed by such expressions of interest. It was our feeling that many of those attending had made it a point to avail themselves of every learning opportunity in this field of study. While, in part, this may be satisfactory for many; for others it represents a fragmented and often times confusing picture of the status of this field. If we wish, this could be likened to another problem, namely the lack of coordination in our programs and plans. We anticipate that the development of this Conference on an annual basis will provide, in some small way, a long-term view of this field and offer a meeting ground and forum for the gathering of interested professional workers and the dissemination of their ideas.

And finally it became apparent that contrary to the pervasive attitude of pessimism and despair which permeates much of the mental health field, such an attitude was not prevalent at this Conference. In large measure, these particular speakers had been chosen because of their unique contributions already made to this field. We suspect that this particular selection of speakers aided considerably in dispelling the notion that we have innumerable obstacles to encounter before significant progress can be effected. As highlighted by the speakers, many obstacles have already been hurdled and the path ahead is not completely uncharted. It is challenging, not immovable. It is possible, not insurmountable; but most importantly, significant gains are being made and translated into action programs for disturbed children.

PETER KNOBLOCK

Syracuse, New York
1965

THE SOCIAL PSYCHOLOGICAL
COMPLEXITIES OF AN
URBAN CLASSROOM[1]

LOUIS M. SMITH

Louis M. Smith has studied at Oberlin College and the University of Minnesota, receiving his Ph.D. at the latter school in 1955. Presently he is Associate Professor of Education and Psychology at Washington University in St. Louis, Missouri. His interests are varied as can be seen in membership in professional organizations ranging from the American Educational Research Association to the Society for Applied Anthropology. At the present time he is keenly interested in social psychological analyses of public school programs, with particular focus on classroom observation and behaviors of the teacher as a decision-maker. He has written numerous articles for professional journals and has co-authored with B. B. Hudgins a text, *Educational Psychology: An application of social and behavior theory.*

Whenever one is granted the opportunity to talk about "problems and prospects" for the next ten years in an area of Education, one should probably resist. As you know, predicting pupil behavior demands considerable ingenuity and hordes of data; predicting the behavior of the "field" presents a different and more difficult item. Perhaps by accenting the "problems" aspect of the theme and by illustrating with a strong personal bias, we can focus upon some issues of mutual benefit. The bias I have, and I offer it with due humility for the enormity of the task, states that the most vital issue today in education, educational psychology, special education, or more specifically, teaching the disturbed and disturbing is the development of a general theory of teaching. By general theory of teaching, I mean a set of concepts with careful nominal and operational definitions, clearly and logically articulated general propositions relating the concepts and logically derivable hypotheses

---

[1]The research reported herein was supported by the Cooperative Research Program of the U. S. Office of Education. Project S-048.

7

capable of verification in field and laboratory experiments. This morning I would like to raise with you some of the excitement, issues and difficulties one encounters in a quest for such a more general theory of teaching.

Initially, so it seems to me, one should hold reservations about this because "theory" is one of the good words today in our field. Slogans and fads come and go. This concerns me in two correlated ways: first, I am revolted by what I call "crest riding," the ability of persons to anticipate each new rolling wave of enthusiasm in the field, to catch the rising swell as a surfer does on the beach, and to ride it for his personal pleasure or gain. Second, when the brief glory of the ride has passed, the particular wave has gone and new ones take its place for the moment. I would hate to see this happen to "general theory of teaching" for the issue is too significant and the returns will not be forthcoming immediately.

In analyzing why the issue seems so significant, a number of reasons come to mind, but two stand out. First, in trying to abstract the major suggestions from books with titles such as "teaching the gifted," "teaching the slow learner" or "teaching the disturbed," I have been struck by either the commonalities residing in teaching in general or the inability of the authors to make a very extended case for the special aspects of their area of endeavor. Second, as I have come to know well over the last dozen years a number of elementary and secondary teachers, I have been struck by the fact that they all hold intensively what they would call a point of view or a philosophy of teaching. In more psychological terms, this is a schema, cognitive map, or *personal* theory of teaching. My experience has been that these maps are often logically inconsistent and helpful more as a rationalization rather than as a powerful analytic tool for solving perplexing classroom problems. In their poorer forms, these personal but general theories of education reduce to a tired series of mutually contradictory cliches about teaching. Perhaps the worst forms of these, in the eyes of the teachers, occur when the cliches are emitted by those of us who carry the title, professor of education.

Concretely, I would like to describe some research we have been doing in urban schools the past few years which we see related to this problem and bias of a general theory of teaching, which has specific overtones for the disturbed and disturbing child, and which generated our topic "the social psychological complexities of an urban classroom."

METHODOLOGY

The most succinct statement summarizing the procedures of the investigation is contained in the sentence, "A year ago last Fall I spent all day, every day, observing *one* seventh grade school teacher and his class of children in an urban slum school." My University commitments were lightened; my days were reasonably free. I attended the public school opening day exercises, faculty meeting, informal daily staff coffee klatches, and daily lessons in reading, writing and arithmetic. It was the most fascinating professional experience I had ever undertaken.

Briefly, two points should be clarified concerning the methodology: one of these concerns what I call the logic of this approach and the other concerns the "how-to-do-it" aspect. Though both of these issues are being elaborated into papers of considerable length, two paragraphs will suffice for our purposes. One of my colleagues has called the approach "the micro-ethnography of the classroom." That has a nice ring to it; it makes what one does sound academic and important. Beyond this, it puts the methodology into the anthropological tradition, with the benefits and liabilities that that suggests. More recently this research orientation has been described by sociologists as participant or non-participant observation. Within psychology the parallels are to be found in naturalistic observation and clinical method.

In short, while the procedures have real hazards, the approach seemingly should not be condemned out of hand for there are a variety of scientists behaving in quite similar fashion. This may seem overly defensive, but I have had considerable self doubts about just what I have been doing. The major purpose I had, beyond seeing concretely what life was like in an area where I had had no personal experience, was to build a model of the events of this classroom. Such a theory would be in the form of hypotheses to be tested by laboratory and field experiments. My results *are* hypotheses, hunches and guesses. Typically one does not produce verified principles with this type of research. If we understand each other here, it will save us considerable disagreement later.

The "how-to-do-it" aspects of the method were these: I made contact with an intraceptive teacher who had some interest in the idea and who then checked with his principal. Later I talked with the principal and other responsible parties in the school and secured their permission. In the class I sat at a table on the side and toward the back of the room. I took copious freehand notes of the events of the class. My concrete focus was centrally on the teacher and his behavior; my conceptual bias centered on social system theory. More particularly, I had just finished writing with Bryce Hudgins an educational psychology text; in this we had spent considerable time with McClelland's personality theory, Homans' conception of human groups and Skinner's descriptive behavorism. Most certainly the ideas from these men selectively guided my perception.

With the pupils, I was introduced as a University teacher who was interested in finding out how children learn, what they find difficult or easy, and what they find interesting. In the day-to-day relationships, as I lived in the class, I never told on them for things they did which the teacher didn't see or for what they did when he was out of the room. I did not pry into their affairs but was always willing to listen and to talk with them. With the other teachers, I was a naive but persistent observer of Mr. Geoffrey's class. I did not go into their classrooms nor observe them teach. As we became friends they told me more and more about what life was like in their school. I tried to listen carefully and to understand the nuances of the latent as well as manifest things they were saying. In general, I tried to stay out of the way of the flow of events. However, I was around as the day-to-day trials, tribulations, joys and excitement occurred.

In the classroom, I kept lengthy field notes of the events of the day. I bought a portable stenorette and dictated long, daily statements of observations and interpretations. These daily records grew to a horrifying quantity. The field notes have been typed into multiple copies. Ultimately these are the raw data processed as we build our models.

The class I observed was located in a metropolitan slum community. The homes mostly were tenements in need of repair. The school had the reputation as "a good school in a difficult neighborhood." The teacher had taught for five years in the building. He had the reputation as a strong teacher and a good teacher. He lived in a suburban, middle-class neighborhood and commuted by car to the school. The children were not too atypical for this community. Of the original 28 children, all but three had tested I.Q.'s below 100. One child had a Kuhlman Anderson I.Q. of 137. Approximately half had failed seventh grade last year and most at some time had failed at least one grade. All but three of the children were white. Many of the children were not born in the city but were migrants from the rural south. Conversations with some suggest that their families were originally from lower socio-economic levels of the communities they left. Many of the children would spend weekends and holidays "in the country" visiting relatives. After the first month of school, a room was closed in the building due to less than anticipated enrollment. Half of the original seventh grade group were replaced with 20 sixth grade pupils. This meant that the teacher taught a split class — approximately 14 seventh graders and 20 sixth graders — for the remainder of the semester. This new group was a "difficult group" in the eyes of the sending teacher. They had been giving him trouble since the beginning of the year. "I can't get any work out of them" were his words. He was pleased to have a different bunch of children.

RESULTS AND DISCUSSION

Today, on the basis of these observations, I would like to suggest three broad issues about which a general theory of teaching must contend. These include bureaucratic authority, functional equivalents, and teacher decision making. The congenial synthesis of these ideas and others such as the development of classroom equilibria, nature of pupil roles and belief systems, formal and informal faculty organization, awaits the completion of the data analysis.

Bureaucratic Authority

For many years now our field has been fighting wars over the pros and cons of democratic and autocratic styles of teacher-pupil interaction and occasionally, when a Rousseauian advocate or client centered counselor talks of teaching we even have skirmishes about a laissez-faire alternative. These discussions blend into curriculum issues, structured versus permissive, and control styles, punitive and nonpunitive. As I observed Mr. Geoffrey, and occasionally other teachers in the halls, and listened to their conversations, I was struck by the fact that they were all authoritarian. As they told me on innumerable occasions, "You have to be with these children." But within the authoritarian approach it seemed to me gross differences occurred. Our notes began to contain phrases contrasting "bureaucratic authority" with "personal or arbitrary authority." By teacher authority, we mean that most of the orders, commands, decisions flow from the teacher to the child and compliance then occurs. Bureaucratic authority implies that the teacher is bound by rules and orders just as is the child; that is, he does not remain totally free or capricious. Also, an element of impersonality enters in; that is, the teacher treats the "offense" of the pupil as against the system rather than against the teacher. As I have indicated, we think bureaucratic authority can be contrasted with personal or arbitrary authority.

Essentially what we mean conceptually is covered in such cliches as "the teacher doesn't hold a grudge" and "the teacher's behavior stresses group or organization goal attainment rather than his own whims or prejudices." An illustration from the field notes, late in the morning, specifies our meaning. The class is finishing a recitational lesson in use of the dictionary.

11:23   Mike is talking to Billy. Mr. Geoffrey observes, hesitates, but does not speak. The conversation is terminated.

11

11:24   Alice says "5 minutes" to Lucille and Richard. She's ready to go to lunch. (They are part of lunch crew.) Mr. Geoffrey comments: "How many are through? Those who are please wait patiently and quietly. Sam." Mr. Geoffrey walks around the room, gives Alice a look. Stops to talk to Sam. (LMS — Can't pick up conversation except something about staying busy, book report, etc. Sam protests that he has finished and ready to give report.) Discussion — not quite banter occurs between Mr. Geoffrey and Sam.

11:28   Sends Richard to board for No. 1. "If you disagree don't hesitate to tell me." Debra No. 2. Finally silence. "Sam, all right that's enough. Turn around. All the way." He does. Benito No. 3. Ernestine No. 4. (These are volunteers.)

11:30   Lunch workers leave. (Alice, Lucille, Sandra, Ernestine.) Terry No. 5, Sandy No. 6, No. 7 . . . No. 8 Stanley; No. 9, "all right Sam." (LMS — This raises another interesting point. The altercation of a moment ago is past. Sam is asking to write — volunteering. Mr. Geoffrey accepts this and lets him.)
(LMS — Relate to Nellie Campbell's categories and H. H. Anderson's.[2] Time interval though brief is very critical. Bygones, etc.)

11:36   Asks for questions.
Sam volunteers for erasing the board. He's granted.
He does erasing with vigor.

11:38   Mr. Geoffrey comments: "All right, listen." (Sam and Donna are excused — apparently because they have repeated and heard it.) Sam gets into "can and may" banter on library book. Mr. Geoffrey reads a poem. (I recognized the bright blue cover of his book, he previously had prepared this while class worked.) "The Son" is title. "Write down what the woman was talking about. Anyone have anything written down?" Mr. Geoffrey checks around. Comments: "that's part of it, almost lost?, that's right," etc.

11:41   Reads again and interlocks explanation with questions and explanations. Sandy sees light, "Oh." "What happened?" "He dies." Second illustration of surprise and joy at seeing the point. (September 10)

---

[2]While we have been dealing here with bureaucratic authority, the observer noted three additional kinds of problems: (1) the difficult to define categories of "Rewarding through social approval" which Campbell (1935) used in her analysis of teacher management of discipline problems, (2) Anderson's (1945) conception of breaking a vicious circle of dominative behavior with integrative behavior and, (3) rudiments of the "process" conception, behavior along a time dimension, which will play such a significant role in the monograph based on the study.

In short, Mr. Geoffrey has had his problems with Sam. In a number of specific ways he's been seeking to obtain Sam's compliance in working on the lesson. Later, when Sam volunteers to go to the board Mr. Geoffrey permits this. Even later when Sam has another request—erasing the blackboard—Mr. Geoffrey allows him to do this.

This kind of episode occurred and recurred throughout the semester. Frequently the pupil request, after the altercation, involved requests on the child's part to leave the classroom for a drink of water or a trip to the restroom. On these occasions the "nonarbitrary" element of bureaucratic authority stood out. Prior rules had been set in the class that trips to the water fountain and the restroom could occur whenever no group lesson or recitation was in progress, when no-one else was out of the room, and when a request was made to the teacher. When the requests came, Mr. Geoffrey, with only a nod, would excuse the child. He too was bound by the general rules. His authority was not exercised whimsically or arbitrarily.

The contrast was highlighted in the behavior of other teachers. One was equally authoritarian in that she directed the class and determined most events which occurred. However, she differed quite dramatically from Mr. Geoffrey. By reputation of our observation, she was known to hold a grudge, to be "waiting for a pupil to make a mistake," and to take pupil rule breaking as a personal offense. In our analysis authority was personal and arbitrary; only the pupil was bound by the rules and the institutional goals. We hope to develop shortly instruments to measure validly these concepts and to move to the antecedents and consequent relationships. We have suspicions that motivation, drop-outs, suspensions and other variables will correlate significently with our distinctions.

Functional Equivalents and Inequivalents[3]

When I first approached the classroom, I carried a host of the current dichotomies: traditional versus progressive teaching, textbooks versus units, class recitation versus individual work, and so forth. Fairly early in the semester I was struck by several recurring events: first, the teacher was a textbook teacher. By this I mean the bulk of the program focused on moving steadily and systematically through texts in spelling, language arts, arithmetic and so forth. The notebooks are replete with statements describing the activity and interaction in dealing with the arithmetic

---

[3]I am indebted to Professor William Connor for first suggesting the viability of this concept regarding another educational phenomenon, alternative modes of training student teachers.

problem on page five, then page six, then seven and so on. In spelling the weekly units consisted of definitions, use of the words in sentences, special exercises and so on. We can pin down concretely the activity of any day during the semester. But after having said that he was a textbook teacher, one misses the larger truth of the classroom if one doesn't say more. For instance, in regard to a second regularity, recitations varied from calling on pupils by moving through a simple up and down the rows, only volunteers, mostly nonvolunteers, to calling on pupils who had looks of confusion. Occasionally this produced some high humor. Early in the semester the teacher checked a spelling test by calling on pupil volunteers. He had turned down several volunteers with the comment, "You've already had one." When the group came to the word "tardy," Mr. Geoffrey called on Sam, an ambling, heavy set, Jackie Gleason type boy. Sam immediately retorted, "Oh, I've already had one." Mr. Geoffrey then commented "I'm giving you this one special." Later when I went back to the notebooks I found that the next four pupils called upon also had received one earlier in the list. The humor introduced in the above illustration proves not to be atypical. The notes contain recurring episodes of "banter," a tete-a-tete interaction in which the teacher and one or more pupils exchange witty remarks. Third, the teacher's behavior involved a tremendous amount of "circulation," i.e. he was on his feet moving continuously from pupil to pupil. This circulating behavior was punctuated with yes's, no's, nods, more vehement expostulations, questions as to sources of answers, and explanations of difficulties.

In summary, by calling the class a "textbook oriented class" one misses the more important point that the pupils are receiving considerable individual and personal help with their learning activities. Functionally, the class is equivalent to many aspects of programmed learning — carefully sequenced materials, active pupil responding and immediate reinforcement. Or, functionally, the class is equivalent to many more informal learning situations wherein humor, pupil volunteering, and individual attention are the keynotes.

Another illustration clarifies the idea of functional *inequivalents*. During the course of the semester two social studies texts were used. As I listened to the lessons, I was struck by the differences in the questions asked by the test authors. In one, the questions were:

1. Why did some European countries seek a westward route to the East? Why did Columbus think he could reach the East by sailing westward? Why did he fail?

2. Why was Columbus' voyage important?

In contrast, the questions of the other text were of this order:

14

1. The Ethiopians were successful (*traders*).
2. The Ethiopians have been (*learning*) from early times.
3. A ruler of the Ethiopians was the (*Queen of Sheba*).

For the moment, I don't wish to enter into a discussion of which questions are better. The point I would make is that the latter accents the recall of fairly specific facts, category one in the *Taxonomy of Educational Objectives* (Bloom, 1957), and the former accents analysis and evaluation skills. Even though both are illustrations of a common approach, textbook teaching, they don't function in the same manner.

This kind of argument — functional equivalents and inequivalents — suggests that we must settle some of the implications of varying levels of abstraction. When one says that two concrete and different procedures have something in common or two supposedly similar events are different we are engaging in the not so simple, but time honored process of conceptualizing. At its best this can move us in the direction of cumulative and more analytic tools which is the essence of any scientific inquiry. At its worst it can move us toward a cynical reductionism — all theories of teaching are "really" theories of psychology and as every psychologist "knows" all psychological theory is "really" physiological. Stephens' (1960) conception of spontaneous schooling has overtones of this.

As we have been saying, at one level, "many roads lead to Rome," the conception is a very simple truism. At another level of analysis, our theory in education makes distinctions which do not exist, or does not make distinctions when they do exist. This spills over in our research methodologies also. The current vogues in the analysis of teacher behavior seldom taps the interdependencies and functional equivalencies in homework assignments and textbook materials which may stress attainment of information while the teacher stresses intellectual skills or vice versa. The teacher may stress information and leave the skill development to carefully drawn homework questions, projects or text assignments. The concept provides an additional implication which suggests items to which the innovator who wishes to improve teaching and learning in slum schools or elsewhere might attend. Merton comments:

> As we have seen, once we abandon the gratuitous assumption of the functional indispensability of particular social structures, we immediately require some concept of functional alternatives, equivalents or substitutes. This focuses attention on the range of possible variation in the items which can, in the case under examination, subserve a functional requirement. It unfreezes the identity of the existent and the inevitable. (Merton, 1957, p. 52)

The unfreezing of the existent from the inevitable opens the discussion of a multitude of other ways, new means, and innovations which can accomplish present manifest ends as well as other latent and desirable objectives.

Teaching as Decision Making

Researchers who use the nonparticipant observed methodology relate insightful experience when the thesis, which lurks in their data, sharply comes into focus. Insight phenomena have a flashing, startling, and exciting quality to the perceiver, even though they may be slowly shaping to the outsider. To me, a major result in this investigation is the hypothesis that the teacher can be viewed from the model of decision maker.

As we looked to more general theory on decision making, we found discussions of fact and value propositions, rationality, alternatives, subjective probability, consequences, effectiveness and so forth.

Teaching often involves doing or not doing something such as tossing or not tossing a chalkboard eraser to a child as a dramatic illustration of a direct object in language. "Choice behavior" is part of the decision maker's conceptual repertory. It is also part of the teacher's schema. Lying behind such a choice are the teacher's objectives in language arts for the morning. Objectives are goals and values to the decision maker. The teacher suspects that such action on his part will startle a few children, provide a concrete illustration of an important concept, and will give him a chance to compliment lightly or tease gently one of the boys for his skill or lack thereof. The decision maker, conceptually, refers to these suspicions as subjective probabilities. The several events which might occur are, to the theorist, consequences. Later, when the children report, within another teacher's earshot, such an incident to their friends, there may occur other events which the sociologists call latent and unanticipated consequences.

Our teacher may not only throw or not throw an eraser but he may call a child up front and rap him on the head lightly but with a flourish, or he might draw humorous stick figure cartoons on the board. In the theorist's terms, any one of these or any combination are alternatives. They, too, have consequences. The consequences have several kinds of probabilities held by the teacher, and we might phrase his behavior as *"subjectively rational."* Theorists might attack such an illustration analytically with such concepts as *objectively* rational, *organizationally* rational, and so forth.

As I watched Mr. Geoffrey toss his eraser and break his pencil, and as I talked with him later about the reasons for his actions, I became enthused about this discovery of teaching as decision making. A number of sub-problems began to fall into place.

The Prediction System

Schematically, a cogent analysis of decision making has been made by Bross (1953). He suggests a model involving a prediction system and a value system. Very simply in his diagrams, the prediction system choices lead to alternatives and alternatives to consequences. The consequences have varying probabilities. Although his diagrams do not indicate them, arrows should run from Alternative A, to the Consequences following from A_2, and vice versa also. The probabilities may be close to zero but they should be indicated.

Similarly his figure should be elaborated to account for latent and unanticipated as well as manifest consequences. Throughout the account in the description of the development of the classroom, alternatives arose which seemed plausible to me as observer. On occasions as I suggested these to Mr. Geoffrey, he would react with an intuitive feeling that this would not be appropriate. As we talked, he would elaborate a variety of consequences which I had only partially anticipated. An illustration of this occurred early in the semester when I raised the concept of "pacing" and the slow speed with which the children were introduced to academic content. The summary notes capture his reaction:

> . . . his statement concerned earlier experience in which he tried to rush the children (and rush probably would be defined as moving them along faster than they would want to be moved by themselves.) Moving more rapidly in his experience has often resulted in not getting very much farther in the long run, and at the same time, frustrating everyone, the children and himself, and creating, as a consequence, several emotional problems in the group. (Summary notes September, 1964)

The Conception of the Ideal as an Approach to the Value System

As we have elaborated, decision making involves what we have called, after Bross, the prediction system and the value system. The latter has presented us with a number of difficulties. In most situations requiring a decision it is impossible to: (1) determine the desirability of each alternative, (2) compare these desirabilities and undesirabilities and combine them into a meaningful summary. Among the many reasons for this, the lack of scales with common meaningful zero points and units is among the most important. In wrestling with this problem, analyzing our own decisions, and attempting to order our data we have found that a model involving a "conception of the ideal" makes tentatively a more satisfactory point of departure.

In the vernacular, this might be phrased "If you had your druthers how would you like things to be?"; or "What do you see as the optimal equilibrium?"; or "What is the best of all possible worlds?". Such a statement implies, as a minimum, the following:

1. An assessment of the desirable "elements."
2. A patterning including an ordering of the elements surrounding their importance.
3. One man's optimal pattern is not another's; i.e. it is subjective.
4. The pattern of one system, e.g. one's job, must be articulated ultimately with other systems, family, self as a person, and so forth.
5. The ideal may change momentarily or over long periods of time.
6. The system may be congruent or in conflict with systems of other individuals, groups, or institutions.

In essence, this involves a careful elaboration of an individual's goals. As value premises these are statements of wishes and desires. The ultimate goals, whether they be a well considered philosophy of life, religious position, or ethical social-political framework, is a statement of first principles, which because they are first principles by definition are not derivable from other propositions. Classroom goals and conceptions of the ideal must necessarily fit into this and relate to it with varying degrees of probability. Classroom ideals must also effect a compromise among personal, group, organizational and community positions.

Combining the Prediction and the Value Systems

In one sense decision making involves a very simple judgment as to whether the prediction system surrounding one alternative or chain of alternatives corresponds more closely to the ideal conception than does the prediction system following the selection of another alternative. Obviously, decisions are not that easy.

To return to our data, Mr. Geoffrey had to decide, after a month of school, which children would be sent to the next teacher and which children would remain with him. As he later commented on the decision, the prediction and value elements stand out rather dramatically:

> I decided to send to her the group I had received at the beginning of the year—mostly repeats from Rooms 13 and 14 and new students who had come in. I kept the other 'natural' group—those who had come to me from Room 16. I did this because the group I sent her was older, etc., than the Room 16 group, and I felt the seventh grade group would fit better with the sixth graders than would the other group. . . . the numbers were okay per the instructions from the office. . . . I was sensitive to what had happened the previous year. I chose the simplest way administratively and one which I thought she would have the least complaints about.

And in regard to the complications arising from the fact that several groups of siblings were involved:

Some of these kids had been together anyway. Since I made the decision by groups I saw no particular reason to make any exceptions. . . . After all, I had both Alice and Richard together anyway, and she (another teacher) had had both Debra and Connie together. All-in-all again, I took the simplest way to a decision—by the groups in which the children came to me.

Strategically, we would hypothesize that the process proceeds more effectively when one frames his ideal of value system *first*. By asking for an organized statement of ends, conditioned by the time, place, and circumstances in which decisions must be made (and this needs elaboration), one introduces what is usually called flexibility and rationality. Then, immediately as alternatives are raised at any choice point, one can compute probabilities of an alternative aiding the attainment of a goal or sub-goal. One of our next research steps will attempt to verify hypotheses in teacher attempts to combine prediction and value systems.

Operationalizing the Decision Making Model

The decision making model has tremendous possibilities, we think, in linking conceptually such diverse influences on the classroom as the formal curriculum guides, the faculty peer group beliefs and norms, and the composition of the class itself — be it lower socio-economic status as in Mr. Geoffrey's case or in programs for the emotionally disturbed, as in the case of most of you, and treating teaching functionally rather than just structurally. To make the conceptual models viable, operational techniques become mandatory. For a long period of time we had considerable difficulty in thinking through concrete ways in which we could implement the model in field research with ongoing classes. While our discovery, if it be that, sounds simple as hindsight, the process of arrival was slow and difficult. The lead we see here combines several elements: first one must establish several "natural" units in teaching — the lesson, the day, the week, the unit of the semester. It is our belief that the unit will vary with a number of conditions: for instance Mr. Geoffrey's spelling program had basically a weekly rhythm within which there were also daily regularities. The independent reading, library books and book reports, had a semester unit as the rhythm.

If we select a single lesson in a subject such as geography we can illustrate further. The model requires that the teacher be quizzed via questionnaires or interviews concerning her goals (the value system) and the means (the prediction system) for reaching the goals in the geography lesson. An alternative, which has the beauty of objectivity and ease of access, is to make the age-old "lesson plan" into a functioning research tool. In Mr. Geoffrey's case, as with many experienced teachers, the lesson plans in geography lay in his head, in the text, and in assignments registered in his "plan book" which all teachers were supposed to keep up to date.

After selecting the unit and obtaining quantifiable statements of plans and intentions the third step, careful observation — with a move toward reliable quantifiable schedules — of the lesson, would then occur. Fourth, post-lesson interviews or questionnaires concerning altered goals and means and cues which suggested to the teacher the need for alterations could be obtained. As a number of teachers in varying situations are studied, verifiable principles should be generated.

Such a mode of research would allow comparisons between school and teacher goals, would begin to clarify our concept of functional equivalents, would move away from an overall "good-bad" assessment in favor of more situationally expressed aims and procedures, and would capture more of the ebb and flow of teaching which many of our analyses have missed up to this time as we have focused on what the teacher does independent of her thought processes or what she thinks, independent of what she actually does. Such research also provides a means of attacking the problems of inservice education and altering teaching in mutually desirable directions.

Additional Implications

With the model in hand, we began to see a number of additional implications into difficult problems. We entitled these: legitimizing the "What do I do?" question, the best of a bad situation, congruence with teacher schema, model of the teacher training product and treating children as decision makers. In a short paragraph I would spell out each of these.

By legitimizing the "What do I do?" question I mean that for many years, in my experience, teachers have been asking the question, "What do I do with this child, this situation, or this problem?" For as many years, in my experience, psychologists and teacher educators have parried the question by remarking "It's impossible to respond to such a question; answers aren't that simple." To their colleagues, the teachers comment about unhelpful experts. The psychologists and teacher educators, to their colleagues, comment about the teachers wanting "something practical," "wanting a push button psychology," or "wanting recipes." One of the major exceptions to the shying away tendency has occurred in the efforts of Fritz Redl (1957) and his colleagues. The hypothesis I would offer is that the decision making model legitimizes the teacher's question. By this I mean there is basic psychological theory in which such a question is not heresy, but in which the question, in its more abstract form, holds a central position. For instance in a literature lesson, "What goals do I have?" "What are the specific ways I can present this material?" "What probabilities of success exist for changed attitudes, for information, for reading skills?" A research-supported theory of teaching will indicate the probabilities of these relationships.

The best of a bad situation suggests another group of difficult problems faced by the teacher. For example, Mr. Geoffrey was faced with the dilemma of giving or not giving homework assignments. Part of his thinking was predicated on such principles as, These children are academically behind for their age and grade; additional work beyond class time is necessary to maintain progress much less to cancel the increasing discrepancy. The kids are apathetic and will do little homework. The parents are distinterested in school and will not support the teacher's efforts. Assignments which are made but not carried out will weaken the teacher's power and control in future situations. As we, Mr. Geoffrey and I, talked about such complexities in assignment making, he would ask, with a twinkle in his eye, what would "the *good* teacher" do in this instance. The "good teacher" was one of our standing jokes of ideal means in the real world and of pat solutions to these difficult problems. The decision model point of view suggests that each alternative or pattern of alternatives has outcomes scalable in desirability as well as probability. On occasion the range is from low or moderately undesirable to extremely undesirable. The solution rests in picking an alternative which, while not desirable in some absolute sense, is relatively more desirable than other alternatives. In the teacher's terms, you "make the best of a bad situation." Such an analysis fosters rationality, suggests pertinent research problems, and lessens the load of guilt carried by the teacher. Obviously one must guard against restriction in alternatives considered and rationalization in logical analysis.

Congruence with teacher schema concerns the consequence of making the model conscious and explicit. When I first raised this conception with Mr. Geoffrey he was skeptical. He found Simon's *Administrative Theory* book not especially exciting. As we introduced appropriate content this skepticism moderated. If it can be established that teachers implicity operate within this framework then we may have an important vehicle for moving from the "real world" to one we might call, on some grounds, more ideal. Specifically, I am thinking here of long, involved discussion that I have had with students who reject Skinner's image of man as it is presented in *Walden II and Science of Human Behavior*, and who have difficulty thinking of classroom problems in behavioristic terms. If the shifts one is trying to make do not demand reorganization of the basic dimensions of teachers' conceptual systems, the probability for alteration and innovation should be higher. This hypothesis needs evidence.

The model provides, for me, a clearer image of the product of a teacher education program and suggests some experiences, role playing, simulation, and successive approximation in classroom behavior, as vital but not currently prevalent. We are planning currently to build situations and problems from our data and present these in our educational psychology classes. We hope this will have a number of affective as well as cognitive effects upon our undergraduates in the preservice program.

Another implication upon which we are working is this — in some contexts Mr. Geoffrey treated the children as decision makers. He acted with them, both verbally and nonverbally as if they had choices, e.g. to attend or not attend, to behave or not behave, to do their work or not. They were held responsible, accountable for their actions. He indicated the consequences which followed such choices on their part and which consequences he had control over — that is which were alternatives in his own repertory. For purposes of the present discussion, I would hypothesize that the conception of the child as a decision maker is a different conception than the child as a product of operant and respondent conditioning. I state this a bit hesitantly for we have just finished an educational psychology text in which we take, in part, a strong Skinnerian bias. Also, I am hesitant in that I have not pushed, as yet, the comparison at any length or depth. On the positive side, it helps me integrate two aspects of the counseling and mental hygiene literature. Ralph Ojemann's (1958) "causality training" and E. G. Williamson's (1950) "clinical counseling" attempt to make clients more rational seem closely aligned with the decision making point of view. Mental health problems, I would argue, are an important dimension of the reality of cultural deprivation in the classroom. Insofar as these psychological positions can be integrated conceptually, they can be drawn upon for help.

SUMMARY AND CONCLUSIONS

In summary, the next decade in educational programming for disturbed children contains a number of imperatives. I have argued that one of these should be movement toward a general theory of teaching. By this, I mean an articulated set of concepts useful in handling the array of problems faced by the classroom teacher. Among the varied ways of approaching such a goal we have found the participant observer methodology to be both exciting and instructive. It puts one very close to the lives of teachers and children. Substantively, we have argued that the theory should have such foci as bureaucratic authority, functional equivalents, and teacher decision making. If time had allowed we would have accented problems in the processes by which the early equilibria are developed, various roles which children play in the class and how this might offer an alternative to the usual conceptions of pupil personality, and special roles particularly relevant to disturbed and disturbing children. We have a strong commitment to moving the ideas toward operations which will permit verificational studies. Finally our analysis has carried more than an implicit emphasis on being useful to the teacher. We see this as an important requisite of applied social theory. In sum, these are a few of the social psychological complexities of an urban classroom.

REFERENCES

Anderson, H. H., and Brewer, J. E. Studies of teachers' classroom personalities, II: Effects of teachers' dominative and integrative contacts on children's classroom behavior. *Appl. Psychol. Monogr*, 1946, #8.

Bloom, B. S. (Ed.) *Taxonomy of Educational Objectives.* New York: McKay, 1956.

Bross, I. D. *Design for decision.* New York: MacMillan Co., 1953.

Campbell, N. *The elementary school teacher's treatment of behavior problems.* New York: Teachers College, Columbia University, 1935.

Merton, R. K. *Social theory and social structure* (Rev.). Glencoe, Ill.: Free Press, 1957.

Miller, G. A., *et al. Plans and the structure of behavior.* New York: Holt, 1960.

Ojemann, R. H. The human relations program at State University of Iowa. *Personnel guid. J.*, 1958, *37*, pp. 199-206.

Redl, F. and Wineman, D. *The aggressive child.* Glencoe, Ill.: Free Press, 1957.

Skinner, B. F. *Science and human behavior.* New York: MacMillan, 1953.

Smith, L. M. and Hudgins, B. L. *Educational Psychology.* New York: Knopf, 1964.

Stephens, J. M. Spontaneous schooling and success in teaching. *Sch. Rev.*, 1960, *68*, pp. 152-163.

Williamson, E. G. *Counseling adolescents.* New York: McGraw Hill, 1950.

COMMENTS ON "THE SOCIAL PSYCHOLOGICAL COMPLEXITIES OF AN URBAN CLASSROOM" By: Louis M. Smith

EDWARD J. MURRAY

Edward J. Murray is presently Associate Professor of Psychology and Director of the Clinical Psychology Training Program at Syracuse University. He is a diplomate in Clinical Psychology and has taken an active part in various psychological organizations. He has contributed a number of articles to the professional journals dealing with such diverse topics as hunger, pain, fear, and conflict and has recently authored a book, *Motivation and Emotion.*

I would like to begin by saying that I am envious of the intensive observational experience that Professor Smith has had. An experience like this can have a deeper and longer lasting effect on one's conceptions than any amount of statistical data. I recall a similar experience of my own when I worked as an attendant in a mental hospital. I had always had a distaste for somatic therapy, and I still do to a large extent, but I cannot forget the strong group spirit and positive atmosphere I observed on a ward of schizophrenic patients being treated by prolonged insulin coma. Professor Smith has emerged from his experience with an intellectual fervor, an intolerance for over-worked concepts, and a skepticism about his own theories. It might not be a bad idea to make this a required experience for all university faculty members concerned with educational problems.

As valuable as this sort of experience is, it is not enough to build the theory of education that Professor Smith so strongly values. Professor Smith has presented us with an inductive base for models, hypotheses, and just plain hunches. The major task of scientific deduction and verification remains ahead. This is not simply a question of adding to the sample of one classroom group but of studying systematic variations in the measurable dimensions that have been suggested. Professor Smith is quite aware of this. We shall all be interested in the research he presents in the years ahead.

Now, I would like to comment on a few of Professor Smith's specific ideas. I was very impressed by his analysis of functional equivalents and inequivalents — genotypical versus phenotypical similarities. The concepts we use in the behavioral sciences are gross indeed. One of the particularly loose concepts is authoritarianism. Social psychologists have already found that authoritarianism is not a simple dimension with all the "good guys" at one end and all the "bad guys" at the other. Extreme rigidity can be found at either end of a scale of authoritarianism or at either end of the political spectrum. Professor Smith's distinction between "bureaucratic authority" and "personal or arbitrary authority" is quite important. It is reminiscent of the studies on frustration and aggression in which it was found that arbitrariness of the frustration was crucial in whether or not aggressive reactions would be produced.

Professor Smith treats the authoritarian issue separately from the idea of functional equivalents and inequivalents but to me it is the best example of how things can be labelled one way but mean something else. Professor Smith has given an example of a teacher who could be categorized as authoritarian but who actually is a warm, flexible person who sees children as unique individuals — hardly a description of a fascist! On the other hand, there may be individuals who label themselves as democratic who are actually extremely authoritarian. I was struck by this the other day in reading an account of prison life in a popular magazine. The author was an anthropologist sentenced to an ultra-modern, minimum security federal prison supposedly dedicated to rehabilitation rather than punishment. The only problem was that no one on the prison staff believed in rehabilitation. Everyone paid lip service to the idea but in practice the prison was run to suit the convenience of the administration, to allay the fears of the guards, and to maintain the subtle destruction of the self-esteem of the prisoners that seems to fulfill some societal need.

This sort of problem has tremendous implications for the education of emotionally disturbed, culturally deprived, and mentally retarded children. Suppose for example that a school decided to set up a special class for emotionally disturbed children. Suppose, too, that a formal decision is made to staff the class with a mature, warm, permissive teacher with experience in handling emotionally disturbed children. The class is to be kept small and homogeneous. A psychologist is to be retained to provide consultation. The principal is enthusiastically for the project. The conditions are ideal enough to make a Professor of Special Education tremble with ecstasy.

What actually happens, though? Things get off to a good start — a properly trained teacher is employed and a class of fifteen emotionally disturbed children is formed. Soon there are complaints that the class is too noisy. The principal solves this by moving the class to an unused room in the basement — a little dingy, perhaps, but far enough away. In spite of this the teacher starts making progress and the principal praises her at a staff meeting. A few teachers grumble that they could do as well with such a small class. Imperceptibly the number of referrals to the special class increases — a hardened delinquent, a hyperactive brain damaged child, and a schizophrenic so badly disturbed that he should be in a hospital. The principal is pleased because he has found a convenient dumping ground for all of his problems but the teacher is disgusted and quits.

The principal has trouble finding a replacement so he persuades one of his *mature* teachers (close to retirement) to enroll for an evening course on the education of emotionally disturbed children and take over the class. Of course, the teacher is a bit rigid but she is mature and experienced. There is another staffing problem in finding a psychologist — fully trained school psychologists are expensive and hard to find. Finally someone suggests a man with a background in physical education who has been giving routine intelligence tests for two years on a temporary certificate. Unfortunately, he has never seen an emotionally disturbed child up close.

At the end of the school year — when the experiment has been declared a complete failure — the principal is an embittered man. "We did everything we were supposed to," he says. "We tried permissiveness, used mature teachers, kept the class as small as we could, had psychological consultation, the works." He adds, "This soft-headed psychological approach is all wet. What these kids need is some old-fashioned discipline." Professor Smith might have a few things to say about the functional equivalencies and inequivalencies in this sort of situation.

I have not been involved myself in the Syracuse Madison Area Project for culturally deprived children. Nevertheless, as I read about its lack of significant success, in the local editorials, I find myself wondering about the gap between the kind of support promised and the kind received, about the theoretical procedures and the actual procedures, about the phenomena that were supposed to be functionally equivalent but were not, about attitudes that were supposed to be new but were functionally equivalent to the old attitudes. Perhaps, later, someone better informed about this than I am can tell us about it.

I would like to move on now to Professor Smith's ideas about teaching as decision making. I think that the analysis of the value system and the prediction system is quite interesting. I find it similar to Julian B. Rotter's theory of social learning. Rotter assumes that the choice of behavior is a function of the values of various goals in a given situation and the expectancies that various behaviors will lead to various goals in that situation. The main problem with formulations of this sort, as Professor Smith points out, is to find methods for measuring values and expectancies. Nevertheless, any progress in making values and expectancies explicit will undoubtedly help in educational planning and in the evaluation of program effectiveness.

In the education of the emotionally disturbed child, it seems to me that a number of goals may be valued differently by different members of the social organization. One goal would be the removal of an emotionally disturbed child from a regular classroom so that the other children can learn more efficiently. Another is to provide an atmosphere more conducive to the educational development of the emotionally disturbed child. Finally, one could view the purpose of the special class as primarily psychotherapeutic — the resolution of emotional problems without regard to educational achievement. Thus, a person with one goal would view a class as successful and another person with a different goal would view the class as a failure. This sort of value conflict could lead to serious administrative difficulties.

It is in this general area of value conflict that I would like to raise some questions about Professor Smith's paper. I do not believe that Professor Smith deals adequately with the subtle emotional and motivational factors in the classroom group. Perhaps this is due to Professor Smith's Skinnerian bias. In my opinion, Skinner's approach is quite superficial — and I say this after years of training in the Skinnerian stronghold of Columbia College. I think Professor Smith may become somewhat disenchanted with Skinner if he pursues his analysis of the child as a decision maker.

I see the classroom group, or any social grouping, as a complex interaction between the personalities of the various participants. In order to understand such a group, one must take into account the motives, emotions, self-concepts, and value systems involved. Let me give an example from Professor Smith's paper. He described Mr. Geoffrey as a good teacher living in a suburban, middle-class neighborhood, commuting by car to the school situated in a difficult neighborhood. The children are from lower class families, many from the rural south. One immediately suspects a clash of values. I once heard that rural southerners have a saying that " . . . too much book larnin', spoils the shootin' eye." I wonder if this clash of cultural values is relevant to Mr. Geoffrey's

27

conviction that the class could not be moved along too quickly. I wonder how much educational progress can be made without finding some way to deal with these cultural value clashes and even deeper emotional factors.

I would like to give you another example from my own research. For the last few years I have been studying the family backgrounds of emotionally disturbed boys of elementary school age. These boys were all having school difficulties and had been referred to the local child guidance clinic. Among other things, we administered Thematic Apperception Tests to these boys and their parents, as well as to normal boys, who were adjusting well to school, and their parents. The TAT stories were coded and scored for aggression, affiliation, and achievement motives. The results suggest that the fathers of these boys have strong aggressive and affiliative needs but low achievement needs. The mothers, on the other hand, are high in achievement. The emotionally disturbed boys are much more like the fathers than the mothers. In fact, there was a negative correlation between the achievement needs of the mothers and sons. There was also evidence of a conflict between the father and mother.

Interpreting a bit, what seems to be going on is that the son is being forced to take sides in a marital conflict. As he identifies with his father he rejects his mother and her achievement values. His school failure is simply an extension of the family problem. It seems to me that the behavior of such a child in the classroom situation would be inexplicable without an understanding of the motivational factors just described.

In conclusion, I would like to say that the sort of social psychological analysis of the classroom that Professor Smith has begun is extremely important for education in general and for the education of the emotionally disturbed child in particular. The concepts suggested by Professor Smith — bureaucratic versus personal authority, functional equivalents, and teaching as decision making are quite promising. In addition, I think it is important to make a deeper analysis of the emotional undercurrents in the classroom situation.

INTERVENTION TECHNIQUES FOR THE CLASSROOM TEACHER OF THE EMOTIONALLY DISTURBED[1]

WILLIAM C. MORSE

William C. Morse is presently a Professor of Educational Psychology at the University of Michigan where he has taught since
1941. As Director of the University of Michigan Fresh Air
Camp from 1945 to 1961 Dr. Morse contributed greatly to our
knowledge of the behavior of disturbed children and techniques
for modifying such behaviors. The author of several books,
including *Psychology and Teaching* with G. M. Wingo, Dr.
Morse is actively engaged in the completion of a text in the education of disturbed children with R. D. Rabinovitch. Dr. Morse
co-authored, with R. C. Cutler and A. H. Fink, the recent study
of public school classes for the emotionally handicapped which
has been published by the Council for Exceptional Children.
Dr. Morse has served as President of the Michigan Phychological Association and is Chairman, State of Michigan Mental
Health Department Task Force on Children's Services.

The use of various processes to change children's behavior, exclusive
of traditional therapy is, of course, not new. However, it took Caplan
(1963) with a term like "intervention techniques" and Redl (1959)
with his concept of milieu to work out an elaborate set of propositions
concerning influence potentials of the situation including both props
and people. In another publication he contrasted the ego oriented
approach with the inner life approach of the more traditional influence
efforts (Redl, 1963). Many have joined in the effort (Goodrich, 1958).

Caplan makes an especial point that the significant intervention must
be aligned to the total life of the child. The implication of this for the
classroom teacher is clear: no matter how well designed and executed
classroom centered intervention processes may be, their impact will be

---

[1]This chapter in expanded form will eventually appear in a volume by Morse, W. C.
and Rabinovitch, R. D. *Education of the Disturbed Child.*

29

limited in scope unless they touch the critical issues in a child's life. In our own work we have used the concept "situational analysis and planning" to embody the broad potentials in ego related and sociological interventions in contrast to traditional "treatment," but this is done with a profound recognition that there is need for both styles of effort, and not either or. We have been surprised both by how much milieu intervention accomplishes with certain children and how limited its effects are on others. The net import of the concept of intervention is to give a high premium to the power of interactions of the pupil with his environment both to induce change and arrange situational prophylaxis. In certain instances it is thought that one begets change through setting up adequate socializing or resocializing influences without resorting to a direct verbal approach to the psyche. This is particularly important in work with children, since here the growth and developmental processes themselves often open up new channels and receptivity for change. Thus, it is that the nature of the classroom environment, the conditions a teacher sets in a classroom, the choice of curriculum and the modes of adult interaction are all matters of primary importance in therapeutic effort. The management of these situational factors constitutes an essential part of the total content of therapeutic education. Each interaction with a condition has a potential for change just as each interpretation might in classical therapy. However, as we intensify our study of these matters, it may be possible to avoid the narcissistic preoccuption with minutia of I said to him and he said to me which has become the subject of some analyses of the nature of the one to one interaction.

Again, an adequate program for helping the disturbed child will make provision for externally focused interventions and internally focused work as well. It is unusual for either alone to be enough to produce the desired changes in seriously disturbed children. The brief survey of classroom interventions which follows does not imply that these will cure. However, until we look sharply and carefully at such environmental manipulations we remain a rank amateur. The present plea is as follows: as we look ahead, can we avoid provincialism or the dictates of over-simplified theory and look rather to a vastly expanded view of the potentials of the special classroom for inducing change.

The two major vectors of classroom interventions, the academic and adjustment areas, are each extensive areas. We have fortunately rid ourselves of the notion that these are mutually exclusive, for as the child operates as a whole, the academic interventions will certainly influence the adjustment elsewhere and vice-versa. Only for the sake of convenience are the two separated.

We start by looking briefly at some possible interventions which constitute the very heart of therapeutic education. While most of these might be subsumed under the general heading of increasing individualization, this very act of individualization has introduced one of the most serious unintended interventions in many special classrooms: it is the intervention of sequential tutoring. To bring about individualization, the teacher frequently rotates from one pupil to the next in turn until all have been "taught" and then the sequence starts over (Morse, 1964). Individual remedial or therapeutic tutoring on a one to one apart from the group is a recognized teaching procedure for the disturbed, but the same method used in the social context of a class is quite another. One could hardly imagine conducting a series of individual interviews in a social setting, yet we assume we can teach this way. If the learning problem is entwined with emotional reactions, such exposure may be most stress producing. After basking in a period of one to one, though more or less remotely listened in on by the group, the pupil is then deserted as the teacher moves on to the next individual. Remember, while one pupil was gratified, the others were looking on from the outside, being asked to wait out their turn for relationship. Most of them demonstrated that they were not up to handling this as they demonstrate by their demanding, interrupting and disrupting behavior, often directed at the teacher, and requiring considerable teacher action. Thus, in the individualization which turns out to be the one difference usually practiced to a significantly higher degree in the special class, there must be a counterbalance since we are involved in teaching groups. As we look at the specifics enumerated below, we are reminded that both individual and group process are necessary in the design of interventions.

Several counterbalancing suggestions can be offered through group interventions. One is through utilizing a group organized curriculum as described by Rhodes (1963) in the project method. There are also integrated several level teaching units which specifically incorporate multi-sensory activities. These will serve a classroom as a group with pupils ranging from the most limited to the very able. A third group intervention process is to organize parallel but discrete learning sequences which are to a large degree self-sustaining for each pupil. Haring and Phillips (1962) propose that each pupil follow his own series of activities as previously planned by the teacher. This individualization (Waller, 1960) is less contaminated by competitiveness than is a series of reading tasks or a workbook or a reader series which imply one single sustained pattern for all. The individual differences are only where one is and how fast one travels on the same educational Cook's Tour. Every pupil has a similar ticket, and differences in location and rate induce a competitive focus. If one were to design a system to equal the tension of sequential tutoring as an inciter of competitive feelings, this one track curriculum would be it.

A fourth intervention designed to draw pupils together is through group discussion about academic affairs. This is not group therapy or even group counseling: it is the use of the group processes to reduce the emotional charge attached to academic work. One teacher had the pupils write about then discuss the "educational machine" they would most like to invent for themselves. There were magic reading machines, writing machines, arithmetic machines and memory machines. As they discussed these, without the teacher resorting to any direct interpretation, it was possible to free up tension by sharing feelings of inability with only a few gentle comments from the teacher. The individual differences were evident and the right of each to his own particular problem reduced negative peer comparisons relative to adequacy.

Another set of interventions takes a cue from a special concept of readiness. Readiness can easily be a tautology: give him lessons for which he is ready and he will do them. Conversely, if he doesn't take to it, he obviously isn't ready! The problem of the teacher is to help the pupil to respond to the edge of readiness rather than bask in easement. How can we encourage responses as close to the capacity as possible? If we misjudge we either delay possible progress or pile up frustration with impossible expectations.

Hewitt (1964) has given us a basis for planning. He points out that some children start out at a primary task level where it is still necessary to appeal to "basic needs" to establish any contact — he uses candy upon occasion. The next level is "acceptance tasks," where the teacher becomes a meaningful person based upon interpersonal relationship. Next some children are ready for "order tasks" where control becomes imposed. Many of these order tasks are school survival necessities such as sitting at a desk and following directions. Next he is ready for "exploratory tasks" using multi-sensory experiences, largely through games, music and the arts. Now he is ready for "relationship tasks" implying the ability to respond through social approval and disapproval since this rests upon a trusting relationship. The next level is "mastery of tasks" as found in the basic curriculum. Finally the child is ready for "achievement tasks" which imply self-motivated learning. It is obvious that, from the guidelines in this theory, we are often planning our interventions as if the child were at level six when he is in reality at level two.

Another set of interventions have as their core the control of anxiety. Certain situations, such as the traditional school setting or content, activate anxiety to the degree that the child cannot handle. Neutralization (Jacobsen & Faegre, 1959) has been advocated in order to skirt tension producing curriculum or conditions. New approaches which are "uncontaminated" and thus do not arouse the negative are built into the design. The dehabilitating emotional component is reduced to an intensity which the child can manage with his coping skills.

Sometimes doing nothing at all (non-intervening if you will) is the most astute intervention technique. For instance the teacher does not respond to such statements as "I can't do it" or "I won't do it" knowing that this signals fear of failure. But, as the child sees he can do some of it, his verbalization is forgotten. For the teacher to have entered into "supportive discussion" might well have crystalized actual resistance. Another process which helps the pupil cope with anxiety is to concentrate on the skill learning as therapy. Hence the "skill therapy" approach. Here the learning act is controlled with great perspicuity so that success will breed success. Short tasks, machine teaching, and the use of easy materials result in hope based upon realistic accomplishment and concrete results rather than teacher praise or encouragement. Skill interventions may be particularly useful when the pupil's interpersonal complications are high but actual capacity to learn is available.

Another intervention which has the encouragement of teaching tradition and operant conditioning (either would be enough today) is the intensification of reward for proper responses. This may take the form of food, teacher praise, stars, freedom for self choosing or whatever. Of course the problem remains as to what makes the telling reward for a particular child at a particular time. If Hewitt is correct, the average classroom has a long way to go in employing gratifications which will really reinforce given levels of readiness.

Particularly important at the present time are specific interventions planned after diagnosis of individual learning inadequacies, following Bateman (1964) and Frostig (1961). Here the attention is to match remediation with problem. All purpose educational aspirins are no longer sufficient: the remedy must be specific. These concepts are well known in seminars and textbooks though seldom actually practiced in the classrooms: in fact it is unusual to find even such a diagnosis in the files.

There are those who feel that the teacher's belief in a given process is more telling than the process itself as an intervention agent. It is the Hawthorne effect in reverse. The real change which one gets using a method is seen as a result of the teacher-pupil relationship, not the specific method. A specialized technique in the hands of the believer is what really counts. This is a quite different view of intervention than that of the precise measure plus specific remedy where method is all and the teacher person is virtually zero. In the years ahead we will see more polemic around this issue, and one can hope, also some research.

There is another set of interventions in the academic sphere which might be termed sympathetically "captivating gadgeteering." Here we can elaborate about reinforcement, multi-sensory avenues, specificity of response and built in reward. But in addition to these sophisticated matters with which we envelop what we do, many of these gadget interventions have a machine attraction. Ours is a machine culture. Most machines have a hidden psychological enticement which appeals to the child ego (and adults as well) on the monkey-like exploratory inclinations which Harlow reports. You command something when you work a machine. You separate yourself into doer and observer when you record your voice so that you can be both producer and critic. Or, in place of hard earned rambling scribbles which you make on a page there are the articulated, uniform, perfect typed letters marching in formation across the page. Movies and TV have a magic aroma at least for the young. They suggest the possibility for excitement to replace the mundane and prosaic. Thus it is that typewriters, record players, tape recorders, machines for learning and films provide gratifications for many disturbed children. They offer the chance for learning and practice without activating a negative feeling about the adult as well. In our experience, however, some children find this "no person to oppose" relatively unuseful since they need to work out the interpersonal aspects first. Learning and relationship are bound together so that the machine alone is dull. Also, continual use reduces the drawing power of gadgets. A disused, expensive piece of equipment certainly constricts administrators.

INTERVENTIONS FOR BEHAVIOR MODIFICATION

As was said, interventions cannot be directed into logical compartments of either academic or behavior because the child organism resists fractionation. Only the adult roles are fractionated. But there are certain procedures which are primarily focused on behavior adaptations rather than classroom academic learning.

First off, we have the intervention dimension based upon the use of authority. We are only so slowly coming to shed the symbiosis of help and permissiveness. Again there is the tendency to polarize the use of power and authority with such approaches as structure versus nonstructure. Such polarization is based upon an assumption one hopes will soon be discarded for once and for all. This assumption is that we can predicate program on the basis of a theory of teaching rather than the diverse natures of children. This moves us to one of the central aspects of effective intervention. Psychologically we can only accept children as we respond in keeping with their particular need systems. Acceptance rests on psychological reality in the child and not the premise of the theoretician. It would take a most simplified view of human nature to suggest a unitary acceptance pattern for all children to be used by all teachers. Those who reject diagnostic study of behavior (though often they may be intense in diagnosing learning problems), cannot develop psychologically tuned acceptance interventions unless by chance. For example, one does not "accept" a psychopath through the same adult responses as one uses in "accepting" a neurotic. Quay (1963) has indicated that different personality configurations will change in response to different interventions. What this means is that on the power dimension which runs from the permissive, choice, non-demanding pole to the highly restricting, and punishing pole, one selects the intervention style which will help the particular pupil rather than preset any response. While no one dealing with classrooms makes a case for chaotic, seductive encouragement of acting out these days, many would advocate a benign flexibility for certain children who are frightened and ready to retreat. A warm, accepting atmosphere is necessary to help the child trust himself and others. The trick is to prevent this from becoming Id for Id's sake, or the pursuit of regression. Such would not be sound psychological acceptance. As we move further, we find many who advocate the imposition of structure for acting out children as an aid in patterning their responses. Some would appear to make this an end in itself, and apply it to all disturbed children under all conditions, a kind of universal molasses in the spring corrective. Since most children in public school setting — and most other disturbed children for that matter — are acting out, and since it is obvious that such acting out must be modulated, there is ample support for reasonable structure applied with a considerable human relationship leavening on a purely symptomatic level. But there are certain children, due to their omnipotent and unsatellized character structure as Ausubel (1954) would say, who require a confrontation with power as exemplified in a most firm, ungiving structure. This is the acceptance they need. The results of this acceptance by confrontation may be unnerving to the uninitiated for after the storm of protest appears a fractured ego in collapse. It has to be put back together and better coping skills must replace those denied (Duhl, 1964). The tendency to hang on to certain children, shielding them from necessary reality, constitutes poor intervention. Chapman (1962) has written of school suspension as therapy and we frequently use temporary exclusion but usually too late and after improper reluctance (Susselman 1962). Just as strict requirements are sound acceptance for certain children, they are contraindicated for others where pathology dictates another style for true psychological acceptance. He may need toleration of certain limit pushing. Again, there can be no intervention without diagnosis.

A fundamental intervention process lies in the teacher-pupil relationship. We know that this is not built upon the child liking the adult per se as much as it is on the child being helped by the adult to solve his problems. A most frequent reason given for platitudinous interventions is that "I'm getting a relationship." After the relationship is solidified, it turns out to be porous and does not support the strain of late demands.

However, if child identification with the adult model is to take place, one most important factor is the empathic response which the teacher develops for the child. Empathic response requires that the teacher understand the pupil's dynamics so that he can read the symbolic nature of the symptomatic behavior. But the teacher does not interpret this behavior to the child or call for a direct discussion which would only serve to heighten the pupil's defensive stance. The teacher acts in a way which will help the pupil deal successfully with the situation in spite of the motivational and even unconscious reasons driving him toward undesirable behavior. This is done without the typical adult taxation of righteous anger, moral interpretation, demands for immediate change, verbal discussion or the like. Redl has spoken of giving the child hurdle help to counter low frustration tolerance, fear of failure and underlying inadequacy without any therapeutic bloodletting. And we should make the point emphatic that in our experience an inadequate self concept is more often at the bottom of acting out than sociopathy. What the teacher does with empathy is to act in such a manner as to alleviate the pupil's tension without exposing his sensitive ego. He is directed into a saving action. In place of telling a pupil he can't tear up his arithmetic paper, or that he can get another and start over if he does, the teacher moves in with a look at the problem and some step by step assistance as the child begins to be overwhelmed by an overload of discouragement. To care about children is a layman's response; to be empathic with children is a high level of professional accomplishment. The professional will respond to the symptomatic behavior, but not as if symptomatic behavior in itself constituted a diagnosis.

There are other times when the issue must be discussed directly. A most needed intervention skill for the therapeutic teacher is a useful manner of talking with children about their behavior when such is appropriate. This cannot be a pseudo therapeutic interview on one hand or ineffective moralizing on the other. The results of our classroom study indicated that most teachers had no way to exploit the psychological content of life events in a way which would foster behavior adaptation. This is an extensive topic and can only be mentioned here, but if we do not develop our skills promptly in this area, we will find ourselves in the hands of the rational therapy persuasion which faces up to life in the front line trenches but without concern for depth of problems or the ethical point of view which a school setting implicitly has to utilize. The professionals working on Life Space Interviewing (Redl, 1963; Long, 1963) are growing, and more applications are being made to the school setting. It has become a primary tool for special teachers.

Of course, it is necessary to work not only with individuals: many of the teacher's problems involve several children (Morse, 1959). And there is the need for the whole group to discuss things together that may not constitute a crisis of the moment. The same interviewing style can be used for this as well. In general, the classroom teachers we studied indicated that they do little of this type of group discussion. This does not mean that there were few group interactions, but they were often in the form of arguments with the teacher serving as policeman, judge and jury. It would be preferable to have the teacher lead group discussion, planned and purposeful. Sometimes films can be used as a stimulus (Smith, 1958). At other times role playing or sociodrama may be the basis. Often an incident can serve as the starting point. It is interesting that we say pupils can learn so much from each other and not all of it bad, and we know super egos are often bright and shining when thinking things through verbally. But we do relatively little to systematically use the group medium. Whether or not we are willing to give pupils total responsibility is yet another question (Craft, 1964; Coleman, 1964).

The whole area of social group work offers suggestions for interventions which can be used by the classroom teacher. If activity group work is used to help disturbed children outside of school classes, why would it not be worth incorporating into the school structure? (Vinter, 1964; Lapidakis, 1963; Eikenberg, 1964). Fortunately, more and more classes are including activity space, but often this is used in a formal way rather than as a place for creativity, release and direct gratification. This points up the fact that education has too often borrowed appropriate interventions from other fields, only to lose the essence by the manner in which we incorporate them into our programs.

Another whole series of interventions lie in the expressive media themselves — art, music, drama and the dance. It is embarrassing that it has taken a current advocate of crawling to remind us that body movement at all levels has meaning for both the normal and the distraught child. The use of art in special classes can extend from formal teaching to encouragement of projective catharsis. Again, the tension reduction can be oblique through the expression itself without interpretation. More extensive use of the arts would help reduce the constricted nature of our classrooms as well as our insights (Berkowitz, 1951). The special classroom for the disturbed must be more than just a very good, cheerful regular classroom.

Close to these are interventions which incorporate the planful use of play, the major occupation of childhood. As Gump (1955) has shown, all games have meaning and role implications. Some work as equalizers, some delegate control positions to the leader and some make the leader the group scapegoat. There are activities that spotlight a particular person when he acts (baseball) and other activities which allow each to be lost in mass action (tug of war). It is also instructive to examine the role the game enforces on the adult manager or bystander. Some games require the teacher to be the umpire, some to watch and some to help. There are rigid games and flexible games. Others have intricate, complete control by rules. Some have individual winners and some sides. There are impulse games and ego games. This too is a long story, but the point is that haphazard game use may produce the reverse of the intended intervention. It has even appeared at times that game selections are straight out of an adult's countertransference reactions from what the selections produce!

There are also curricular content interventions which may have importance for the classroom teacher's efforts to change behavior. Ojemann has developed material for causal thinking through content material for all ages. Bibliotherapy may be used in a similar manner. There are lists of stories for every type of a problem including the delinquent. A new set of primers has been published which deal directly with the fostering of the self concept. Discussion of one's own problems as depicted in literature certainly is an educational therapy, but it is not likely to happen with Dick and Jane, or the overall moralistic approach which has been found to infuse readers. Two cautions should be mentioned. There is some question about making the modern trend of a reader like life when life has been as brutal as it has for some pupils. The other caution is in thinking that every moment, every word or every act of every day should be exploited clinically. One hopes for most of the time being spent as if the child has no problems when the conditions will so permit.

There is as yet too little work done with the adolescent, especially the school alienated adolescent. Perhaps this will change with the poverty program emphasis, but past experiences indicate that anything we do will require a long hard pull. Many of these youngsters will not be made over into conforming, happy, regular students regardless of our efforts. Some indeed need additional socialization, but after that where do we go? The world of work for many youth is the eventual therapy, and nothing significant is likely to happen until this takes place. The work world gives meaning and structure to life: the sooner it can be utilized the better are our chances. The educational therapy will have to be organized around "money oriented" activities in the work world (Ethridge, 1958; Bond, 1962). It offers a new intervention channel if we are up to it.

Even in this brief recital a word should be said for monitoring the more esoteric interventions which are often missed entirely or dismissed because they are iconoclastic rather than because they have no value. Take the work of Slack (1960). Delinquents were paid to talk into a tape recorder and to take tests. He found a sequence of change and opened contact with hitherto impossible cases. Of course he paid them to talk, and this constitutes a role reversal. As everyone knows, teachers and therapists should be paid for their helping. How we chose to spend a dollar is a critical intervention issue. A few teachers are trying procedures similar to Slack.

If we are going to help children we may have to try many new things. Social workers learned to reach out of their offices. We may find we must reach out of our classrooms at times. The concluding plea is for more flexibility and excitement in our work. If we learned anything in our national survey, it was that things were often commonplace and even dull — except for unwanted child induced excitement. Classrooms can become places of constant exploration and innovation.

REFERENCES

Ausubel, D. P. *Theory and problems of adolescent development*. New York: Grune and Stratton, 1954.

Bateman, B. Learning disabilities — yesterday, today, and tomorrow. *Except. Child.,* 1964, *31* (4), 156-169.

Berkowitz, P. and Rothman, E. Art work for the emotionally disturbed pupil. *Clearing House*, 1951, *26*, 232-34.

Bond, R. Work as a therapeutic medium in the treatment of delinquents. *Amer. J. Orthopsychiat.,* 1962, *32*, 846-50.

Bower, E. The modification, mediation and utilization of stress during the school years. *Amer. J. Orthopsychiat.,* 1964, *34*, (4), 667-674.

Caplan, G. Opportunities for school psychologists in the primary prevention of mental disorders in children. *Ment. Hyg.,* 1963, *47* (4), 525-40.

Caplan, G. *Prevention of mental disorders in children*. New York: Basic Books, 1961.

Chapman, R. W. School suspension as therapy. *Personnel and Guid. J.,* 1962, *40,* 731-32.

Cohen, R. E., and Grinspoon, L. Limit setting as a corrective ego experience. *Arch. gen. Psychiat.*, 1963, *8* (1), 74-79.

Coleman, J. C., and Hewett, F. M. Open-door therapy: a new approach to the treatment of underachieving adolescent boys who resist needed psychotherapy. *J. Clin. Psychol.*, 1962, *18* (1), 28-33.

Craft, M., Stephenson, G., and Granger, C. A controlled trial of authoritarian and self-governing regimes with adolescent psychopaths. *Amer. J. Orthopsychiat.*, 1964, *34* (3), 543-554.

Duhl, L. J. Crises, adaptive potential and the school. *Psychol. Sch.*, 1964, *1* (4).

Ethridge, D. A. Work: a treatment for all disabilities. *Amer. J. Occup. Ther.*, 1963, *17* (1), 16-18.

Eikenberg, J., and Webb, A. P. A group counselling approach to the acting-out preadolescent. *Psychol. Sch.*, 1964, *1* (4).

Frostig, M., Lefever, D. W., and Whittlesey, A. Developmental test of visual perception. *Percept. mot. Skills*, 1961, *12*, 383-94.

Goodrich, D., and Bommer, D. S. Some concepts about therapeutic interventions with hyper-aggressive children. Part I, *Soc. Casewk.*, 1958, *39*, 207-213; Part II, *Soc. Casewk.*, 1958, *39*, 286-292.

Gump, P. and Sutton-Smith, B. Activity setting and social interaction. *Amer. J. Orthopsychiat.*, 1955, *25* (4), 755-760.

Haring, N. G., and Phillips, E. L. Educating Emotionally Disturbed Children. New York, McGraw-Hill, 1962.

Hewett, Frank. A hierarchy of educational tasks for children with learning disorders. *Except. Child, 31* (4), 1964.

Jacobsen, S., and Faegre, C. Neutralization: a tool for the teacher of disturbed children. *Except. Child., 25,* 1959, 243-46.

Lapidakis, J. E. Activity therapy program: for emotionally disturbed children. *Amer. J. occup. Ther.*, 1963, *17* (1), 22-25.

Long, N. J. Some problems in teaching life space interviewing techniques to graduate students in education in a large class at Indiana University. *Amer. J. Orthopsychiat., 33* (4), 1963, 723-727.

Morse, W. C. Working paper: training teachers in life space interviewing. *Amer. J. Orthopsychiat., 33* (4), 1963, 727-730.

Morse, W. C., and Small, E. R. Group life space interviewing in a therapeutic camp. *Amer. J. Orthopsychiat.*, *29* (1), 1959, 27-44.

Morse, W. C., Cutler, R. L., and Fink, A. H. *Public school classes for the emotionally handicapped: a research analysis.* Washington, D. C.: Council for Exceptional Children, 1964.

Myers, D., and Goldfarb, W. A study of parental perplexity in families of schizophrenic and normal children. *Amer. J. Orthopsychiat.,* in press

Quay, H. C. Some basic considerations in the education of emotionally disturbed children. *Except. Child.,* 1963, *30* (1), 27-33.

Redl, F. The concept of therapeutic milieu. *Amer. J. Orthopsychiat.,* 1959, *29* (4), 721-27.

Redl, F. The life space interview in the school setting workshop. *Amer. J. Orthopsychiat., 33* (4), 1963, 717-719.

Rhodes, W. C. Curriculum and disordered behavior. *Excep. Child.,* 1963, *30,* (2).

Slack, C. W. Experimenter-subject psychotherapy: a new method of introducing intensive office treatment for unreachable cases. *Ment. Hyg.,* 1960, *44,* 238-256.

Smith, C. C. Using films in group guidance with emotionally disturbed socially maladjusted boys. *Except. Child.,* 1958, *24,* 206-09.

Susselman, S. The contribution of physical restraint to the understanding of other forms of intervention during psychotherapy. *Amer. J. Orthopsychiat.,* 1962, *32* (2).

Vinter, R. D. and Sarri, R. C. Group work in the public school: a fresh approach. *Soc. Wk.,* in press.

Waller, S. The library method of study as applied to problem classes. *California J. Sec. Educ.,* 1960, *35,* 334-338.

INSTITUTIONALIZED DISPLACEMENT AND THE DISTURBING CHILD

WILLIAM C. RHODES

William C. Rhodes received his Ph.D. from Ohio State University in 1953 after receiving his A.B. and M.A. degrees from Emory University. He is presently on leave from Peabody College, where he is Professor of Psychology, to serve as Assistant Chief, Child Mental Health Section in the National Institute of Mental Health. He is a member of the American, Southeastern, and Tennessee Psychological Associations. He has published a number of articles in professional journals, including a series of recent papers focusing on analyses of community institutional patterns influencing programming for disturbed and disturbing children as well as curriculum considerations for disturbed children.

The presentation of the following thoughts and ideas is not intended as a statement of the way things really are; nor are the proposals offered here intended as the only possible explanation of some of the human and social factors considered. They are presented merely as a systematic interpretation of a set of events with which you and I have to live and work.

THE THREAT-RECOIL CYCLE

There are three reciprocal human forces whose confluence provides an important psychological binding for community life. These three forces are fear, power, and illicit behavior. The structural representation of these three human forces in the community will be specified in this paper as the public sector, the power sector, and the exile sector. When we think of the way in which these three sectors relate to each other through their major identifying force, we might think of the power sector as the protector, the public sector as the protectorate, and the exile sector as the threat-provokers.

We can begin to understand this psychological centrifuge of community life by examining the cyclic phenomenon of community recoil from illicit community behavior. The threat-recoil phenomenon itself has been observed by all of you. The recoil interpretation, on the other hand, is my own construction of the phenomenon, and therefore, will need to be carefully described and explained.

The community recoil phenomenon is quite simple. Over and over again, you and I have observed the national preoccupation with, and anxiety over, specific kinds of illicit human behavior. One year it may be juvenile delinquency, another year it may be mental retardation, and a third year it may be emotional disturbance. The same kind of shifting behavioral concerns can also be observed at the level of the state and local community. Community leaders and community professionals may raise a hue and cry over school drop-outs one year, while a year later they will be aroused and agitated over the increasing prevalence and incidence of alcoholism, and so on.

Within any single recoil cycle, we can observe a gradual community awakening to a behavioral threat. We see an accelerating build up of concern and agitation over this particular illicit behavior. There is a rapid transmission of alarm which ripples throughout the community. More and more people, more and more community leaders, become involved. Next there is a flurry of community actions and reactions. New programs are created. New protective mechanisms are raised between the general public and the group producing the illicit behaviors. Then gradually, over an extended period of time, there is a noticeable diminution of actions, a gradual fading of agitation and a slow dissolving of community alarm over the particular illicit human condition which provoked it. And almost before this cycle has completely faded into the background of community life, a new threat is building. A new source of illicit behavior is provoking the community, and a new threat-recoil cycle is in the making.

In this threat-recoil cycle we are witnessing the confluence of fear, power and illicit behavior. Illicit behavior triggers widespread fear. When the fear has risen to sufficient proportions in the community, it spirals upward along the pyramidal track of the power structure. The power sector then intervenes between public alarm and illicit behavior. It mobilizes community agencies and resources and maneuvers these between the public sector and the provoking sector. It thus assumes the role of the public good, and the public quietly subsides.

The behavioral threat involved in each recoil cycle is usually defined in terms of the language of some existing socializing agency. The public may borrow the language of social welfare to define one threat, and the language of education, legal-correction or mental health to define another. For instance, acting-out behavior which involves violation of other people's body or property rights can be defined in legal-correctional terms as "delinquency," in mental health terms as "character disorder" or "sociopathic behavior," and in educational or social welfare terms as "maladjustment." The public is dependent upon the language systems developed by these agencies to describe what is threatening it.

The cluster of events and the general climate at the time of the occurrence of the threat usually determines which of these agency languages are most likely to be used to define and describe what the threat is. For instance, if there is a particularly dynamic and well liked psychiatrist in a community at the time that a wanton sexual attack is committed, and the newspaper had just completed a series of expose articles on the condition of the local mental hospital, the psychiatrist is likely to be asked to define the meaning of the sexual attack. In this situation, the language used in the recoil cycle which follows from the sexual attack is very likely to be the language of mental health.

The provoking behaviors, therefore, will be given additional meaning (even superfluous meaning) in terms of the concepts, and language, and interpretations of human behavior which the various socializing agencies have built up over the years.

However, no matter which language is chosen by the public sector to represent a particular threat in a recoil cycle, the various socializing agencies will translate the provocative behavior into its own language terms, its own concepts, theories, technologies and its own operational patterns. The community consensus on the name of the recoil focus will thus be redefined and redistributed across the medley of human service concerned with the behavioral affairs of the public.

The public is very fickle in its choice of terms and agencies. It shifts its interest and commitment from one agency to the other. At one time it may favor the language and agency patterns of mental health, and at another time, it translates all of its alarms into the language of education. Its shifting affections, however, are limited to the range of institutionalized agencies which exist in our culture. Currently, educational concepts have high appeal and usage.

In spite of the seemingly random nature of the recurrent flurries of public alarm, there does appear to be a regularity and a pattern in threat and recoil. Threat and recoil is institutionalized. The society has separated itself out into differentiated parties or community sectors to enact a social ritual around threat and recoil. The factions are conceptualized within this paper as the power or protector sector, the alarmed or protectorate sector, and the alarming or exiled sector which produces illicit community behavior.

The ritual which they enact is like a plot in a play. The threatening sector produces its illicit behavior. The public sector flees from the illicit behavior and into the protective circle of the power sector. The power sector activates the socializing agencies and maneuvers them into position between the alarmed public and the threatening sector which has now become tabooed. The public sector then begins to calm down and turns its attention to a new source of threat.

THE PRECIPITANT — THE THREAT-PROVOKERS

The community threat-recoil cycle can begin with either overt illicit behavior, or with simulation of the behavior. Simulation is a term used in a very special way here, which will be made clear a little later.

The precipitant or nexus of the cycle are individuals who elicit provocative behaviors or who exist in one of the many human states threatening in our culture. This could be an alcoholic, a drug-addict, a retardate, a sexual deviant, a delinquent, a psychotic, an underachiever, etc. Individuals existing in any of these states, and producing any of the behaviors associated with that state are rejected from the mainstream of social life. As long as they exist in this state and until there is adequate retribution for their illicit behavior they are relegated to a tabooed caste. This large group makes up the exiled sector of our society. The largest single contributor to this group seems to be the lower class of our society.

When the threat-recoil cycle is precipitated by overt illicit behavior, the quality of the cycle seems to be influenced by certain characteristics of the behavior. For instance, the intensity, the extensiveness, and the duration of the recoil seems to be determined by such behavioral characteristics as: (1) the frequency of occurrence in a given period of time, (2) its location in the hierarchy of community taboos, (3) the intensity of the commission of the behavior, (4) its degree of visibility in the open community, (5) its geographical location and distribution in the community, (6) the drama of its circumstances.

A very dramatic occurrence of even a single instance of illicit behavior is sufficient to precipitate intense recoil. A teen gang killing of a rival gang member on the steps of a church or a school yard is enough to set off a cycle. The killing of a priest or rabbi in an attempted mugging can also produce such a cycle. The senseless and horrifying assassination of President Kennedy by a man whose history included early diagnosis by mental health specialists is enough to set off such a cycle. Senator Ribicoff's bill in behalf of services for emotionally disturbed children is very likely to have widespread congressional and public support, since he ties it to this abhorrent event.

Lacking the condition of a dramatic single occurrence, an outbreak of delinquency will produce repercussions commensurate with how frequently in time the behaviors occur, how widespread they are in the community, the intensity of their commission, the strength of the community taboo against the particular behavior committed. A rapid series of teen-gang atrocities, occurring in various sections of a city will be likely to arouse strong recoil and rapid counter-actions within the community. An outbreak of sexual abuse of children will produce extreme community alarm and reaction because of the importance of the taboo which this behavior violates.

Visibility also seems to be an important determinant of the threat-recoil cycle. Unless such non-visible illicit behavior as suicide, sexual perversion, or child-abuse is made visible, or called to the community's attention, they are not likely to create community alarm even though the behaviors themselves are very high in the hierarchy of community taboos. However, if the behaviors are called to the community's attention, they too will produce the typical threat-recoil cycle. The act of directing attention of the community to these behaviors can have the same effect as more directly visible illicit behaviors. This act of attention direction to non-visible illicit behaviors is being called "simulation" in this paper.

Simulation has become a responsibility of the professional and the politician in modern-day society. They are responsible for continual monitoring of social life to detect and warn of potential threat. Simulation, therefore, is a professional and political interpretation of the nature of threat toward which the community should direct its concern. President Johnson's emphasis upon "poverty" is such a simulation. It is a conceptual representation of a threat; it is an interpretation, several times removed, from a visible behavioral threat. However, it has the same effect as a direct threat. Here, we can observe the same type of community recoil and community action.

Emotional disturbance in children is another symbolic interpretation or simulation which carries with it the same type of threat to the community as direct assault in the streets might have. It produces the same type of recoil and the subsequent ripples of community agitation and community action as more direct and more visible precipitants. The alliance of professional and politician have assumed the constant function of monitoring the community and arousing concern over potential threats.

The community will, in turn, pressure the professional and politician coalition for protection against this threat.

The process of simulation of behavioral threat has become as effective as the direct appearance of illicit behavior in arousing community alarm and producing protective community action. As mass communication methods have improved and as the transactional recoil process has become institutionalized in the community, simulation has become a more and more significant factor in the social order.

THE PROTECTOR SECTOR

We have now moved into a description of the protector sector as it becomes engaged in a community threat-recoil cycle. In discussing the precipitant behavior, we were discussing the threatening sector, or that sector of the community which produces illicit behavior. In discussing simulation, we have turned to a discussion of protective actions and the protector sector of the community.

The people involved come from two segments which make up what I have called the "protector sector" of society. These two segments are: (1) the decision making or power segment (particularly decision makers in the judicial, legislative and executive branches of government), and (2) professionals and agencies allied with government in shaping and regulating human behavior to fit the pattern of social requirements of the public sector. These are made up largely of the systems affiliated with education, legal-correction, social-welfare, and medical mental health.

These two segments of the protector sector represent the machinery of defense against threat. The protectorate, or public sector turns to this coalition as it recoils from provoking behavior in the open community.

Whether the precipitant is a direct expression of illicit behavior or a simulation of such behavior, community alarm is contagious and spreads from person to person and group to group. As the ripples fan outward and spiral upward along the pyramidal track of the power sector, the alliance of power and agency sources are engaged.

At the present time, for instance, we are finding ourselves swept into the undertow of the powerful tides of concern over emotionally disturbed children. We are finding this topic to be more and more on the agenda of panel discussions, of public meetings and of exposure through the communication media. Influential legislators at the state and national level are conferring with influential professionals who are characterized as experts in this area. State and national legislation are designing blueprints for vast action programs of treatment and reclamation of such children.

In the power sector's response to public alarm over "emotionally disturbed children," we are witnessing a general process in any threat-recoil cycle. The standing contract between power and public is being renewed and strengthened. The bases of power are being replenished. The chief decision makers are given additional public mandate to take action, and to use public resources to protect against this threat.

Furthermore, in response to public alarm over the emotionally disturbed child, the ties which bind socializing agencies and government into a single protective force are also being replenished. The health, education, welfare and correctional agencies which are responsible for mediating between society and individual behavior are activated anew. The whole apparatus which these agencies maintain for converting individual urges to approved social expressions is being infused with new energy. Within the interlock of government and agencies we see varied negotiations and varied claims to leadership against this threat. There is bartering and bargaining. There is marshalling of concepts and ideas. There is interchange of position statements. There are compacts and agreements. Finally, a consensus of sorts will be obtained, a decision will be made, a program will be mounted.

Here, in relationship to this one threat, we can see the prototype of the transactional processes which take place between government and agencies when a threat-recoil cycle is in progress. We can examine the function of the threat-recoil cycle in refueling the interlocking machinery of government and agency. We also can observe the engagement of power and public as alarm mounts and instigates the recoil process.

THE PROTECTORATE

The public sector, or protectorate, is made up of the vast mass of individuals who constitute the base-line group of our society. It is constituted largely, although not entirely of the "middle class" population. The middle class is most vulnerable to loss of social and economic status and therefore more cautious and circumspect with regard to its own behavior.

There are many ways in which this public sector could be described. It could be described as a social, an economic, or as a psychological unit. However, there is more heterogeneity in this group as a social or economic unit, than as a psychological unit. Therefore, from the threat-recoil frame of reference suggested in this paper, we might describe this group as the most successful segment of society in both dodging and detecting public taboo and threat. It is the group which stays out of trouble and, therefore, carries greatest weight with the trouble-handling machinery of the society.

If we merely enumerate a few of the threat-provocations which have activated major threat-recoil cycles, we begin to have a vague idea of the catalogue of negatively ladened categories in our society. The gross categories of mental illness, mental retardation, delinquency, suicide, child neglect, drug addiction, sexual deviance, socially maladjusted, social withdrawals, culturally disadvantaged, underachiever and drop-outs, are illustrative of this point.

If I can be permitted to generalize from this type listing and more subtle forms of illicit behaviors which we all know, it can be proposed that the vast array of behaviors which are threatening in our culture, and the endless possibilities for tabooed forms of human existence, makes successful performance in the community a very precarious endeavor. This is true even for members of the culturally advantaged groups. There are so many cultural reefs upon which a member of society can run aground, so many unmarked social lines upon which the individual can lose his balance, so many undesirable classes that he can be sur-reptituously nudged into, that only the most skilled can traverse this difficult terrain.

The group which is publicly free of taint has to be highly competent in detecting and diverting any appearance of threat. It is a type of com-petency which calls for rigorous and meticulous training from the earliest years. The individual, in order to maintain his place in this group, must be highly successful in warding off any association with publicly rejected classifications and publicly rejected classes.

In this accomplishment, the individual has to develop high sensitivity in detecting cues and signals of threatening characteristics in himself, in others and in surrounding circumstances. The individual must also de-velop skills in minimizing such cues in the presentation of himself, and in his private living which influences this public presentation. He must, in other words, orient a major segment of his life around threat-avoidance.

In order to become selectively sensitive to detection and emission of such cues, the individual has to master the data-bank of threats which the culture has built up over centuries. He has to learn and incorporate this vast catalogue within himself and to become skilled in detecting even the most obscure specimens of the catalogue.

It is against the standard of this group that all the other threatening groups are measured and defined. Their consensus determines what is outside the realm of acceptable behavior. Their trained recoil locates and exposes the threat provokers. Their joint appeal for protection, or their composite acceptance of the offer of protection from power and agency groups, specifies which individuals and which groups will be classified as threatening.

The individual not only has to play many roles in his life, but he finds himself surrounded by many shifting exigencies and undergoes many changing internal states. In order to remain in the acceptable class, therefore, he has to spend a great amount of time and energy in monitoring threat, and coping with the danger it presents.

Let us take the single category of "emotionally disturbed," for instance; there are so many states of being, so many conditions of behavior and such a multiplicity of definitions of this category, that one finds it quite difficult to set up criteria for exclusion from the group. Even the most serious term, the "mentally ill" has no single definition or no clear cut characteristics. There is certainly no scientific consensus regarding who has it and who doesn't have it. I can refer you to several reviews of the professional literature dealing with the definition of this concept which conclude that there is no agreement as to what mental illness is. And yet, as a category, this term arouses powerful emotions within the public resources.

Let us look at the multiple ways in which a person can slip and fall into this category. We can find endless possibilities for picking up such a label. A psychiatric opinion can accomplish this. A psychological test battery can determine it. A group of one's peers or of one's supervisors and superiors can do this. A public consensus can class an individual as disturbed. A legal process can decide this. A voluntary or involuntary involvement with a particular agency channel or process, such as being hospitalized in a mental hospital or seeking psychiatric help can do this. (And if you are a mental health professional, a serious disagreement with the dogma of your professional group can accomplish the same categorization.)

With this example of the single category of mental illness, and an awareness of all the other categories always open and possible for any member of the community, let us return to our general statement. The protectorate, involved in the threat-recoil analysis presented here, could be thought of as the individuals most skilled in avoiding threatening classifications. The standard public sector of the community would be comprised of the individuals most skilled in restraining or concealing the appearance of threat. They are skilled in projecting themselves in such a way that they do not arouse composite anxiety in other community members. At the same time, they are the individuals who are most selectively sensitive to threat in others. They are the individuals who most frequently detect and respond to threat and they are the most frequent users of the systems and devices which the community has developed to monitor and protect against threat.

Let us hasten to add that I am sure that this large, solid group also makes many positive contributions to the social fabric. They also have many characteristics, skills and ways of being which are constructive and non-reactive to threat. However, let us remember that the same thing is also true of many in the multiple groups which threaten us. Therefore, we might say that the normative group which makes up the great public of our communities are safe from rejection and exile not only because of their valued and positive characteristics; but also because they avoid exposure of disturbing characteristics and behavior. Their distinguishing social competence is threat-avoidance.

PSYCHOLOGICAL RECIPROCITY

In my opening statement I said that the psychological binding of the community consists of three reciprocal forces whose confluence provides the psychical centrifuge of community existence. I named these three forces fear, power and illicit behavior. The structural counterparts which I separated out of the social fabric were the protectorate sector, the protector sector and the exile sector.

I would like to carry my analysis, and my somewhat arbitrary construction, one step further. I propose that these three sectors are psychological collaborators. Each of them plays out, in the open community, one of the roles of straining contenders in each of us. One sector can be viewed as complementing the other in a perpetual, inter-active charade of the quarrel between the claims of the individual against the claims of the culture.

The sectors represent man's ceaseless struggle to reconcile these contending claims, and his periodic effort to resolve his dilemma by trying to escape either himself or his culture. There is a constant strain of what he is against what he ought to be. The strain is increased by the fact that although the measure of "ought-to-be" shifts and changes with each historical period, the culture seldom permits any of these measures to be dropped from its depository.

Through time, the culture has banked an overwhelming accumulation of such measures of man. The accumulated burden is intolerable for many of us. This burden, interacting with man's vast repertory for possible states of being, and his depthless capacity for fear, has made life in the community a labored and perilous passage. There are so many things that each individual *is* that he *ought not be*. In his lifetime, he lives so many experiences he ought not live, if he obeys the tyranny of the cultural repository. As an individual he is rather helpless before this repository. There are no institutionalized means for periodic re-examination of, or challenge of the functional utility, for community life, of any of these archaic deposits. Therefore, it remains a vast, indiscriminate mass of human taboos, which he must carry and live with.

I suggest, therefore, that much of what we observe in the threat-recoil cycle reflects the institutionalization of a basic psychological dilemma faced by modern man. This psychological dilemma is brought on by the contradictions between the nature of man, on one hand, and the silting up of culture's taboos against various expressions of that nature, on the other. Having institutionalized this dilemma, we perpetuate it.

INSTITUTIONALIZED DISPLACEMENT

The protectorate is the bellweather group of the society, largely middle class, which has spent a life-time learning the burdensome accumulation of man's psychocultural history. Each of the separate items in the vast collection is charged with emotion. As tabooed items, they are particularly laden with fear. And yet, because of the nature of man, each one of the illicit behaviors or states of being can, very easily, be exercised by each and every human organism. The individual who has transferred these out of the storehouse of culture into his own memory bank is particularly conscious of this possibility. Therefore, he carries around within himself not only a burdensome load of knowledge about these taboos, but he is also carrying the loaded threat of behavioral tendencies associated with each. His actions and potential actions are, to this extent, fraught with danger.

The threat-provokers, (to a large extent lower-class), play a particular role in this order of things. They act as a lightning rod for the internal threats of the public sector or protectorate. As a group they have not amassed the vast lexicon of dangers, nor have they amassed the vast skills for parrying them. They are more likely to express all types of behaviors available to the human organism. This is especially true since many of these behaviors are naturally pleasurable or produce immediate gratification.

Their acting-out of illicit behaviors and tabooed states expresses openly a threat which is constantly trembling as a potential in the repertory of the threat avoider. It breaks the tension of the counter-poised possibilities within the threat avoider; the dangerous possibility and human tendency, on one hand, of expressing some form of illicit behavior himself; and on the other hand, his built-in replica of the ever-present physical and psychosocial restraint and retaliations of the culture.

The breaking of the taboo and the commitment of the illicit behavior by someone else allows him not only momentary relief from tension, but also allows him to shift the locus of the threat to the external source.

It is much easier to counteract it, and contain it out there where it is detached from oneself. It can thus be displaced and managed. It can be subject to the mechanisms of social behavior shaping and regulation created for this purpose. This apparatus involves the coalition between power and systems such as legal-correction, social welfare, education and mental health.

In turning to the power sector, the threat-avoiding public sector seems to be seeking to add authority to its own limited capacity to counteract the danger both without and within. The authorities will respond because their power is based upon the consent of the protectorate. Power itself is a relationship. It does not exist without a protector and a protectorate. In our society, one of the bases of power grows out of the substance of threat and recoil.

In a way, therefore, both the power sector and the public sector have a certain amount of dependency upon the threat-provokers. The threat-recoil cycle is both an emergency valve and a source of fuel for the total social apparatus devoted to such cycles. It feeds the continuity and growth of programs, agencies and professional fields, it offers temporary relief to the public sector, and it helps renew the bases of power in communities, states and federal government. This interactive social mass, therefore, has a natural tendency to perpetuate itself.

Let us turn from conjecture now, and take a look at the processes and apparatus engaged by threat and recoil.

In an identifiable cycle, such as that maintained by our current concern with emotionally disturbed children, we can point to the various elements of society which become involved.

There is the generalized public and their lay associations and civic organizations. The communication media of newspapers, radio, television, magazines and public addresses are also involved. These media spread the communication so that more and more people become informed and concerned.

When there is sufficient shared concern, at the grass roots level, power groups and government groups become involved. The legislators draw up bills, the executives throw the weight of the administration behind the bills and the judiciary hands down rulings and interpretations of the bills.

The behavior management systems of legal-correction, social-welfare, education, mental health, etc., are involved. Their disciplines or professionals outside the official government agencies submit advice, opinions and interpretations. They help define the nature of the threat and offer suggestions out of their professional knowledge. Their knowledge, and their training, lodged primarily in their university bases are supplemented and supported by public support and public funds.

The official agencies embedded within the government structure or partially financed by government, through public funds, are then designated as the action arm to contend with the threat. They have new sources of funds available to them and new mandates for programming.

And now we come to an important sequela. Once the program swings into action, it is rarely, if ever, called to accounting. The public does not ask for a reckoning from the program agency with respect to how much of the socially dangerous behavior has been reduced or prevented. The public continues to move to new threatening fronts, but it does not evaluate progress on old ones.

Even where there are such evaluations it appears to have little effect on programs which have been brought in on the tide of a previous threat-recoil cycle. A negative report, indicating either that (1) the program is not affecting the behavior that brought it into being, or (2) that the agency cannot produce any evidence that it is influencing the behavior, is usually ignored. One of the conclusions which can be drawn is that the public feels protected anyway, and does not press for more than this.

Let us ask ourselves a question. Have the few reasonable evaluations of the results of special classes or child guidance clinics, or correctional institutions or welfare programs had a discernible effect on the programs for disturbed children? Are they curtailed, or changed as a result of these?

Furthermore, even though we have not demanded evidence regarding the effectiveness of specific measures or ways in which the established behavior-management agencies handled previous threats, we will, nevertheless, support the use of the same ways or measures in contending with a new threat. The evidence is certainly not in the house with respect to special classes for the mentally retarded. And yet, this is education's answer to the problem of the emotionally disturbed child. Mental health's answer is more child guidance centers.

These are some of the reasons why I have conjectured that the whole threat-recoil process may be largely a displacement phenomena. We displace the threat from ourselves to others, from inside ourselves and our own unstable compromise with the culture to those who are least able to defend against threat.

PRACTICAL CONSIDERATIONS

With respect to the concern that we have for emotionally disturbed children, we should ask why we have built up this level of interest and activity. We should try to be more specific about who these children are and what it is we want to do for them or for ourselves. We should separate out those who are disturbing to us because they do not fit our system and our way of working, and those who really need our help. We should examine the school system and see if there are ways of changing it other than, or in addition to special classes, which will allow the child to function as he is, and still learn and develop. How many of our standards for what the child ought-to-be as a pupil are archaic? How many of these could we eliminate and thus reduce the number of children whom we now think need special treatment?

Do we really need this new pigeon-hole for children in our school system? Do they really have to be separated out, identified as a special group, and handled outside our regular educational stream? If so, we should begin to look at our entire regular-education endeavor. The number of children requiring "special education" is growing at an accelerating rate. Isn't it beginning to appear ridiculous that such a large proportion of the school population has to be placed in special categories so they can have an adequate developmental program not provided by the regular educational enterprise? Is there something wrong with our whole concept of education? Is it really an instructional program conducted by instructional specialists? Or, have we already gone a long way in converting schools from instructional centers to developmental centers? Do we need to divorce these two functions into separate agencies, or do we need to integrate them more fully and plan more systematically for the special needs of all children?

Does each socializing agency in the community have to set up separate facilities and separate competitive programs for emotionally disturbed children? Already, we are building separate strongholds of vested interests in education and mental health programs for disturbed children. When the current training programs for special educators of disturbed children release their first wave of degree people we should see further escalation of program development in special education. Will these vie with mental health? If Senator Ribicoff's bill or one like it is enacted into program will it establish still another vested interest stronghold?

These are the kinds of questions we should ask if we are to make something more than a massive round of meaningless activity out of the threat-recoil cycle associated with disturbed children. The perceived threat of disturbing children should provide something more than fuel for the functional autonomy of the threat-recoil-action apparatus. It should do more than provide a booster for the continued revolving of this social mass within the cycle of its own orbit.

We should ask ourselves what is wrong with our present socializing institutions. If we do have so many categories of people who do not fit our present social systems or present society, shouldn't we ask ourselves what is wrong with the systems or the social matrix of the systems? At the same time, shouldn't we question ourselves about our periodic and changing flurries of excitement over first one behavioral condition and then another? Shouldn't we at least question the validity and utility of these cycles?

SUMMARY

Let me try now to summarize the ideas expressed in this paper and some of the ties that bind them.

I took a brief look at the recurrent flurry of nationwide, statewide or community-wide agitation over varying kinds of divergent human behavior. In summarizing the regularity of these waves of agitation and subsequent social action, I described the phenomena as a threat-recoil cycle. I tried to separate out the various human forces which lend energy to this cycle and proposed that fear, power and illicit behavior were actually interactive in precipitating, propelling, and maintaining the cycle.

In examining the sequence of events within the threat-recoil cycle, it appeared to me that illicit behavior triggered off fear in the public sector, which then turned to power sectors for protection and decision about action.

Certain socializing agencies, associated with varying levels of government, such as social-welfare, legal-correction and mental health are then mobilized. Their mobilization also involves the mobilization of the professional groups and associations allied with these agencies.

As an explanation for the cycle of public agitation over varying illicit behaviors, it was proposed that this stems from the contradiction between the claims of the individual as a human organism and the excessive claims of the culture.

It was suggested that there has been an historical accretion within the culture of restrictions upon human behavior. This accumulation has put inordinate demands upon individuals to avoid behaviors and states of being which are tabooed by the culture. There are intermittent social reinforcements, both positive and negative, for conformity to this vast cultural lexicon. Divergence frequently brings retribution and classification in one of the exiled or tabooed groups.

Every individual has the capacity and the drives for expression of the full spectrum of behavioral possibilities which are tabooed by the culture.

Many members of the culture, however, spend much of their lives in dodging these behavioral pitfalls. They learn the vast catalogue of cultural taboos and the skills involved in avoiding threat in themselves and in others. However, for the sanctioned group, there is tension created by this constant danger of allowing some cue or signal to slip out. The expression of tabooed behavior by others offers one form of relief, or even vicarious release from this constant vigilance. It brings this behavior out in the open through the person of someone external to the self. It is much easier to manipulate, contain and work on behavior when it is thus explicit and divorced from the self.

At the same time, it is recognized as threatening and is feared as such. The power sector and its capacity to deploy and manipulate socializing agencies is appealed to for protection. We thus, have the beginning of a threat-recoil cycle.

The intervention of a program or agency between the threat and the public is enough to allay public anxiety even though this may accomplish nothing more with respect to the illicit behavior which brought it into being.

Having presented this analysis, a number of questions were raised with respect to our current concern over emotionally disturbed children.

THE ROLE OF EDUCATON IN THE REHABILITATION OF THE EMOTIONALLY DISTURBED CHILD

HARRY KROHN

Harry Krohn is presently Supervising Principal of Hawthorn Cedar Knolls School, a residential center for emotionally disturbed and delinquent girls and boys. He has also served as a teacher and guidance counselor at this center. His A.B. and M.A. degrees were granted by New York University with the latter degree taken in the area of guidance. His previous positions included Director of the Curative Workshop for Veterans Administration in New York City, educational consultant to the Jewish Board of Guardians, and the New York State Department of Education.

In November 1964, all chief school administrators in New York State received a memorandum from the Division of Pupil Personnel Services which included a section on the emotionally disturbed child. In essence, the memorandum pointed out that all school administrators had been notified in May of 1964 that Chapter 945 of the Laws of 1964, amended article 89 of the Educational Law by making education for the emotionally disturbed child mandatory rather than permissive. The law is to be effective July 1, 1966. The memorandum quotes the law as follows:["An emotionally disturbed child means a person under 21 years of age who has been determined to be emotionally disturbed as a result of an examination made by a qualified psychiatrist and a qualified psychologist or by an approved clinic, and who is not capable of benefitting through ordinary classroom instruction, but may be expected to profit from a special education service or program."]The memo also mentions the fact that "the Bureau for Physically Handicapped Children has been working with local school districts since the passage of permissive legislation in 1959 in the development of suitable programs and services for these children."

One might now ask the question — why has it taken so long for the educational community to mandate special educational programs for the emotionally disturbed child? Programs for the blind were established in the 1800's. Special institutions for the care and education for the hard of hearing have long been incorporated in the provisions of the educational laws of our state. Programs for the physically handicapped were spurred on by the skills and techniques developed during the two great wars. As educators, we moved in quickly when it became apparent that, regardless of how severely crippled a child was, he could benefit from special educational programs. For the past two decades, the investment at the local, state and federal levels in developing skills and techniques in the field of mental retardation has proven once again what can be accomplished by a total effort. Research into the etiology of mental retardation has been helpful to the psychologist, the teacher, and curriculum specialists; children once assigned to the human scrap heap as uneducable and untrainable are today being serviced by programs in communities throughout the country.

I would like to repeat the question I raised before — "why haven't programs for the emotionally disturbed child received the same attention as the other special programs?" Why indeed has it taken so long for the community to finally place the responsibility at the door of the local school district for the education of these children? In examining the aforementioned groups one notes that they have one common characteristic, namely, their obvious and unmistakable helplessness. Another characteristic is that each of the other areas of exceptionality can be placed in categories which are quite easily defined. Vision and hearing tests are simple to administer and the results are conclusive. The physically handicapped and the mentally retarded can also be placed in fairly definitive categories for medical and educational purposes. Another important factor which I believe is true of these groups is their wish, to a greater or lesser degree, for assistance in helping them to overcome their limitation. After the first flush of anger or hostility on the part of the handicapped person toward the teacher, it is possible for the two to work together toward a mutual goal. The goal is naturally to help the handicapped person to adapt to his environment by fully exploiting his healthy faculties.

Now, let us look at the group on whom this conference is focused. The emotionally disturbed child has also been called the emotionally disadvantaged, the emotionally retarded, or the emotionally damaged. Attempts by the psychological and psychiatric disciplines to place these students in neat diagnostic categories has, at times, contributed more to confusion than clarity. The term schizophrenia is so all encompassing that it has little value as a diagnostic term descriptive of behavior. As if that were not problem enough, we have childhood schizophrenia, adolescent schizophrenia and adult schizophrenia. Character disorders, primary behavior disorders, neurotics, adjustment reaction to adolescence, are all diagnostic terms used to label the emotionally disturbed child. Certainly it is quite different from the neatly systematized methods used by the other exceptionalities in defining illness or limitation. The symptom picture presented by the emotionally disturbed child is rarely interpreted by the adult as that of a helpless individual in need of assistance. Let me hasten to add, however, that emotional disorders are as crippling in their effect on the child as are the other illnesses, particularly when it comes to constructive activities. However, the people he comes in contact with often see him as an aggressive, hostile, threatening child, more to be feared than loved. Whereas in the other areas of exceptionality, the child in his helplessness seeks the counsel and advice of the adult —in most instances the emotionally disturbed child rejects it and the adult, in turn, rejects him.

Let me also point out that initially, programs for the emotionally disturbed child were planned for young children only. Programs for preschool and elementary school children were established by agencies in the New York area many years ago. Parents of seriously disturbed children, who were excluded from the public schools, founded the League for Emotionally Disturbed Children in an attempt to provide suitable education facilities for their children.

These children began to exhibit extreme forms of bizarre behavior at a very early age, and enrollment in public school programs so exacerbated their behavior symptoms that they had to be removed from school. The combined efforts of the mental health clinics and the schools concentrated on a program of research and curriculum planning in an attempt to interrupt the abnormal emotional developmental processes. These programs were begun in the nursery, kindergarten and early school grades where remediation would prevent further intensification of the emotional disorders. The psychiatric disciplines had a great deal to contribute since much of their research into the causes of emotional illness had been focused on the early stages of childhood development. The educator, however, was most familiar with the developmental processes of the normal child and therefore was faced with a task for which he was inadequately prepared. His approach was to modify and adapt the traditional program to the needs of this special group. The self-contained classroom, the non-departmentalized program, the techniques used with kindergarten and early elementary school children were easily adaptable, the emphasis on group living and group activities seemed to be a natural for the elementary school teacher. The ability of the teacher, usually a woman, to provide some of the essential emotional climate of the warm, accepting, and at the same time limiting female, was known to be of immense therapeutic value to this group. The infantile behavior could be dealt with in the classroom situation because the emphasis was on behavioral change and adjustment rather than educational achievement. Since the child's sphere of interest and action at this young age is limited to concern about self and the few adults that he comes in contact with, the classroom setting became an important part of the child's daily life. Much has been done in the area of special programs for these young children and I am sure that in the next decade, the behavioral scientists and the psychiatric profession will provide additional aids to the education of these children.

The children that I would like to spend the rest of the time discussing are those who are considered emotionally disturbed and who range in age from 13 to 18. These are the children we find in our junior and senior high school programs. The difference between the emotionally disturbed child who is in the pre-puberty and latency period and the adolescent disturbed child is tremendous. The normal adolescent, if indeed one does exist, has often been described as a young person who goes through temporary spells of psychosis. He has to cope with a rapidly developing body, newly emerging aggressive and sexual drives, increasing social and educational demands from his peers as well as the adult society. He is constantly confronted with the questions of: Who am I, what am I, and where am I going? His sphere of action, instead of being confined to the home and the classroom, begins to encompass the community at large. He is asked to live up to adult standards and demands, while at the same time he is dealt with as an immature, irresponsible child. He has to make peace with the fact that much of the adult world around him is not what the adults say it is. He must constantly grapple with the world as he sees it. The adults demand that he live up to an ethical and moral society that he, the adolescent, sees nowhere around him; the world, as he often sees it, is fraught with distortion, rationalizations, immorality, and fraud. The adult often boasts of his antisocial activities in the presence of the adolescent; however, if he participates in such activities he is reprimanded or severely punished.

In a world full of so many inconsistencies how indeed does the adolescent survive this period of his life and move on into adulthood? His home environment, the relationship with his parents and siblings is crucial to his development. Attitudes toward others and his own self-image are a reflection of these early relationships. The support and

61

understanding he receives from the home in time of stress, due to anxiety, fear, and uncertainty, helps him develop emotional maturity so that he can cope with these problems. The children in our secondary schools who are emotionally disordered frequently come from homes that failed to provide the emotional climate conducive to good emotional development. This, I am aware, is an over-simplification of the problem and I am aware of the multitudinous factors such as health, heredity, etc., that also affect the child, but I wish to focus on this area because I feel that the school has a very important role in reversing the pattern where the problem results from a pathological home situation.

I would now like to take a closer look at this adolescent and describe some of the problems he presents to the school and to himself. The symptom picture is usually complicated by the fact that his adaptive behavior is reactive to a complex of pathological stimuli. As educators we see the child as poorly motivated, an underachiever, or a behavioral problem. It has been my experience that many of these problems do not appear until the student enters the junior high school program which, agewise, is coincidental with the onset of adolescence. Although much has been said about the trauma that the child experiences in transferring from an elementary school to a junior high school program, I feel there is some lack of understanding of the severity of the trauma. After six years of schooling, where much emphasis is placed on social behavior with academic achievement secondary, the student is now confronted with a situation where the reverse is true. The bright problem child often has devised means for succeeding in the elementary school without having established good work habits. Errands for the teacher, participation in class discussions, etc., ofttimes were sufficient to carry him thru his early school years. He is now placed in a situation where he must meet with five, six or seven different teachers each day, with the focus on achievement. The pressure for grades becomes all important, and the previously learned techniques of the pleasant smile, proper grooming, participation in class discussions, errands, now prove ineffective in his drive toward scholastic achievement. A sampling from case records of other factors that most frequently affect the child's functioning in school are:

1. Conflict in the home between parental figures.
2. Inconsistent handling of the child in the home.
3. Unreasonable demands made upon the child.
4. Lack of moral and ethical values in the home environment.
5. Intense competitiveness between siblings.

6. Parental rejection because the child never measures up to the parent's image of what his child should be. (The most brilliant, the handsomest, the best behaved, etc.)

7. Lack of structure in the home which the adolescent needs but always seems to fight against.

8. Absence of substantial adults that he can identify with.

9. Lack of confidence in himself.

If the child looks to the community for a foundation upon which to build, what does he see?:

a. Love thy neighbor, providing he is not black, yellow, or of another religious sect.

b. Law and order is essential to our way of life except in Selma, Alabama; Philadelphia, Miss.; Dallas, Texas; New York City, and Chicago, Ill.

c. Petty thievery frequently results in severe penalties. Conspiracy by large corporations to defraud governmental agencies results in jail terms of 30 days with 10 days off for good behavior.

I could, if I wished, go on and on, but I am sure you are as familiar with the inconsistencies in our world as I am.

Now let us turn to the school and examine what this disturbed child might find there that he could use an anchor. Will he find the answers to the physical and emotional drives that are plaguing him? Not very likely. What about his social studies courses which emphasize wars, materialism, broken pacts, etc? Certainly there is little here to identify with. The imprisonment of Galileo; the despair of Woodrow Wilson; the pauper's grave of Mozart; the assassination of Kennedy are incidents of despair rather than hope.

At this point one might legitimately ask if all the aforementioned contribute to emotional disorders how come so many manage to maintain good mental and emotional health? I can only answer by stating that the difference between the normal and abnormal is quantitative rather than qualitative. We have all been subjected to negative as well as positive experiences and some tend to cancel out the other. The greater the number of negative experiences the more likely the tendency toward emotional disorder. The following illustrations I hope will further clarify this point.

Psychosomatic Symptoms

The upset stomach and nausea, resulting from extreme degrees of emotional tension is familiar to all of us. That an employment interview can cause sweating and stomach cramps comes as no surprise to many of us. The rubbery legs and dry throats that one is subject to when he appears before an audience may even affect seasoned performers. Meeting deadlines of one sort or another creates pressure that often take the form of headaches. Children who are living under the stresses and strains of a pathological home, a frustrating school experience, and who are unable to function in their own peer groups, may constantly be at the mercy of psychosomatic aches and pains. Many of these youngsters compound their school problem by being absent so often that they are considered school truants. When they do attend school, they often become ill in response to particularly stressful situations and have to leave school. Extreme cases may become phobic about school and are usually placed on home instruction.

Poor Impulse Control

All of us have students in our classes who, from time to time, do things that evoke from us the statement "boys will be boys." However, we are also familiar with the student who is a constant source of irritation because he refuses to follow the school rules, disregards classroom decorum, annoys his peers who are sitting close by him, and challenges the authority of the teacher. Such continuously poor control certainly doesn't evoke the same comment "boys will be boys" but rather — "he seems to be a seriously disturbed boy."

Poor Concentration

We have all had experiences where we were unable to focus or concentrate on the task at hand. This frequently prior to a significant event or just following an event that evoked intense feeling either of happiness, fear or anxiety. In most instances, we are well aware of the causality of such experiences. Can one concentrate effectively in class when he knows that that afternoon the new car is to be delivered? How can one concentrate on the discussion at hand when father, mother, or some other close person is being operated upon this morning? The emotionally disturbed child, however, is constantly responding to incidents and events of the morning, of the moment, and of the future. I must also point out that this is not a deliberate attempt on the part of the child to avoid becoming involved in the class activities, but rather an uncontrolled overwhelming invasion of his mental processes.

Social Maladjustment

The emotionally disturbed child is unable to function appropriately in a group situation. This may take the form of misbehavior, bizarreness,

64

aggression, or withdrawal. The underlying causes for such behavior are usually multi-determined. One may speculate as to the causes and come up with the following:

   a. His wish to destroy the classroom decorum because he cannot cope with the intellectual demands.

   b. An expression of anger toward his classmates whom he sees as sibling substitutes.

   c. His expression of anger and aggression toward the teacher whom he sees as a parent substitute.

   d. His need to be important, to be the big shot, to be the "rock."

These are but a few of the many reasons that may be responsible for the child's behavior.

Underachievement

These children are usually unable to function at or anywhere near their intellectual potential. I have known children who, later on in life, were able to test in the above average to superior range, who during their early adolescent period were unable to function above dull normal range. This area of malfunctioning is most frustrating to the educator because it is extremely difficult to determine the basis for the malfunctioning. It is also true that the usual remedial techniques are ineffective with these children.

The poor reader assigned to a remedial reading teacher sees her as the demanding mother and, therefore, he fails her at every turn. The student who resists the teacher who is trying to help him organize his notes and schedule his study time more effectively may see the teacher as the compulsively rigid adult against whom he is rebelling. The girl who cannot function in American History because her father was killed in World War II and the boy whose father pleaded with him to "learn to read before I die" are two examples of why some students are unable or unwilling to learn because of special meaning in the content of the subject matter. They make up the army of "dropouts," and medical suspensions.

Now that the emotionally disturbed or emotionally handicapped, or emotionally deprived, or emotionally maladjusted, or socially maladjusted child has, to some extent, been identified, what has the community been able to provide for him? In the past, they have been looked upon as students who should be removed from the school because "they prevent others from learning." They have been labeled as lazy, disinterested, uneducable, and apparently the only solution satisfactory to all involved was to remove them from the school situation. In some instances, depending upon local laws, the child was removed from the community and placed in a training school, state hospital or residential treatment center. The prevalent point of view was that these children were somehow not the responsibility of the educational community. As an educator who has been working in this special field for the past 25 years I have had to grapple with the educational problems of these students since I was unable to pass the problem on to someone else. I will not bore you with a lengthy history as to my experiences in working with this type of child during that time, but let it suffice to say that I have come to the conclusion that these children are educable, they wish to learn, they can be motivated, they will give up their antisocial behavior — that in the final analysis their one wish is to be able to function like other children. I must also make it clear that my point of view is not necessarily one that is acceptable to all or to even the majority of educators in this field.

1. I believe that a school program for emotionally disturbed children of the extreme nature that I have described above, must be designed specifically for their needs. We must move away from the concept that a modification of the normal school program is suitable for these children. I strongly advocate the establishment of a centralized secondary school for these students that would embody the latest in architectural design. Consideration has to be given to traffic patterns, recreational areas, lounge areas, etc.

2. In a large school system, it might be feasible to have a wing where such a special school could be housed. Actually there might be some advantages where this is possible in that the transition from this special program to the regular program might be easier. Since this is not feasible in the small school districts throughout the state, I would see a centralized school which might come under the jurisdiction of a BOCES program.

3. Regardless of where the school is located or what its relationship is to the total school district program, I feel it should be administered and supervised by personnel specifically trained to work with these students. This, I believe, is crucial. In too many instances when special programs are housed within schools or where modifications have to be made for these children, the administrators see this as a burden which is not rightly theirs.

4. The teaching staff should consist of personnel specially trained to work with emotionally disturbed children. Once they are on the job, they should also be involved in ongoing training seminars, specialized curriculum committees, and should be encouraged to give leadership to extra-curricular activities so that they can see their students both in a

structured and somewhat demanding situation as opposed to a less structured and somewhat less demanding activity. We will spend more time later on the training of teachers.

5. Classes should be smaller in size than what one is accustomed to finding in the ordinary school but still should not be so small that it loses the flavor of a class. I would say that no less than seven and no more than twelve should be used as guidelines in establishing classes. Those classes which tend toward the remedial should of course have a lower figure, whereas classes with children whose achievement level is on a higher level might tend toward the higher numbers. The total school population should be limited to a maximum of 250 students.

6. In terms of numbers, a school with 250 students is considered a very small high school. However, when one realizes that we are talking about classes that average 10 rather than 30, our school must be compared with the 750 student normal school. Curriculum tracks both in the academic and vocational area are essential. The individual program designed for each child must take into consideration his intelligence, his emotional makeup, his social adaptability, etc. In designing such a program, they may include high level academic courses as well as low pressured industrial arts courses where he can relax and use up excess emotional and physical energy. Flexibility in program assignments is essential so that changes can be made to meet the student's needs.

7. Remedial and tutorial services must be readily available. Most of these children, by the time they reach secondary school, are educationally retarded. If they are to be sustained in school they must be helped to overcome their educational deficits. Their low frustration tolerance and feelings of inadequacy can be overcome if these services are available when the student is experiencing difficulty in class.

8. There should be a complete psychological workup on each child upon admission to this special school. There is much that we can learn from psychological tests that will contribute toward good educational planning for these children. The program should include educational, clinical and interest tests.

9. There should be a sufficient number of guidance counselors so that no more than fifty students should be assigned to a counselor. These counselors have to be trained in the area of educational and vocational guidance and should be skilled enough to deal with these students when they act out or present unusual types of behavior. In addition, for the more seriously disturbed youngsters, there should be available treatment services of a continuing nature. Psychiatric social workers or psychiatrists should be included in any plan for special schooling. Provision should also be made for family counseling wherever that is in-

dicated. In many instances, unless intensive family counseling does take place, little, if any, change of a permanent nature can be hoped for. As I indicated at the beginning of this presentation, much of the problem may stem from family attitudes toward the child's functioning in school. If the family is unable to deal realistically with the limitations, where they exist, much of the effect of the school efforts will be wasted.

10. A special school should have many extra-curricular activities of an enriching nature. Many students who are having difficulty finding success during the school day, might begin to experience success and achievement in extra-curricular activities. Many underachievers who cannot function in a rigid structured classroom, find avenues of expression in the arts, dramatics, writing, etc. If these experiences are satisfying and successful they may be able to bolster the student while he is going through a difficult time in his other school activities.

I would like now to return to the role of the teacher in the special school. First and foremost, he must be one who is well versed in his subject area. He should also be well organized and be able to use whatever visual aids are available. When one is confronted with a class of emotionally disturbed children, any one of whom might explode at any time, he should not have to struggle with the subject matter or the techniques of good teaching. Next in importance and probably most difficult to come by, is a greater understanding of himself as an individual and a human being. He must be aware of his own limitations and his own drives. He must be trained to deal with difficult situations as objectively as possible so that his own problems do not become intertwined with those of the students. He must react in response to the classroom situation and to the conditions of the moment rather than to anxieties, fears, frustration, uncertainties of his own past personal experiences. He must be able to communicate strength and structure without punitiveness and anger. He must have an awareness of the problems that each child in his class is struggling with so that he can interpret the student's behavior realistically. He must have an understanding of group dynamics so that he can work toward developing positive and constructive group experiences. He must be able to provide structure without rigidity.

The question which naturally follows is, where can such teachers be found? The universities and the community will have to bear the burden of training such teachers. Special courses to provide greater insight and understanding of these children will have to be provided for by the university. The community will have to develop in-service training courses so that teachers who choose this specialized field can participate in training seminars where they can discuss the problems that arise in their classrooms. The supervisory staff will have to be chosen from the ranks. There is nothing more devastating to a teacher of emotionally disturbed children than to have a theoretician, who has had no experience in working with these children, supervise him. The supervisor must be totally aware of the kinds of problems that the teacher struggles with, those resulting from the difficulties of the students as well as those that stem from the anxieties and uncertainties of the teacher himself. In my school, I have developed a position called the counselor-supervisor. This person has responsibility for a counseling load of no more than 50 children and is also responsible for the supervision of teachers. In this way, he and the teacher are involved in a joint effort to help each child, and the success or failure of each student is a product of their combined efforts. Finally, there is the role of the principal or chief school administrator. It is his function to create a climate where all disciplines can work closely and harmoniously. He must be knowledgeable in the ways of the children and be understanding of the staff that struggles with them from day to day. He must supervise and counsel the supervisors so that they can deal objectively with teachers and students. He must create a climate where new ideas and techniques are encouraged.

The learning process requires one essential ingredient on the part of the student that is crucial to any educational process, namely, his wish to learn. The student overwhelmed with emotional problems usually has his desire to learn destroyed by the time he arrives in the Junior or Senior High School. I believe the special school that I have proposed may revive this desire for the following reasons:

1. The curriculum, especially designed to deal with the educational and learning deficits of the student, will provide sufficient opportunities for success instead of failure. They have such a poor image of themselves that unless the process is interrupted they are defeated before they start. The curriculum must be flexible enough to allow for exploitation of those areas of the student's interests and abilities that are intact.

2. The teacher will see himself as a specialist in the education of the emotionally disturbed child. His energies will be invested in devising new methods and techniques in working with these students. In the regular school the teacher regards the deviant child as an unnecessary burden and often communicates this to the student. The teacher's attitude is understandable in light of the pressures he is under, namely, to teach 25 or 30 students and to cover a specified amount of work in a given time.

3. In this special school the student will feel part of the total student body. He will be aware that others are struggling with problems similar to his. In the normal school he is usually an outsider and unable to

participate in group activities with his peers.

4. The atmosphere and structure of the school will be such that certain types of deviant behavior can be effectively handled without destructive effects on the student or the program. Here again the staff, because of their training, can view a situation objectively and, therefore, are constantly aware that deviant behavior is symptomatic of a much more serious problem. The experienced teacher can, therefore, confront the student with his behavior and in so doing use an incident as a learning experience.

5. Because of the various problems that these students present it would seem to me that only in a special school that is extremely flexible can realistic goals be set for each individual child. In the community school many normal children conform to programs that are unacceptable to them but do so in order to please society and their parents. These children do not have the motivation to please anyone and can only be worked with if they are given realistic goals that meet their needs and wishes. This may mean deviation from standard type curriculum tracks and modifications of certain curriculum areas which would be totally unacceptable in the normal school.

6. The student in this special school will be seen as he really is rather than as he would like others to see him. Delinquent and bizarre behavior is usually a coverup for emotional disturbance. Most adults in dealing with these children compound the problem by reacting to the surface behavior. The child is then committed to fulfilling the image. Another factor is that the student would rather be labeled delinquent than emotionally disturbed or "crazy." If teachers are aware that the delinquent facade is a defense their reaction to the student's behavior will be more thoughtful and deliberate.

7. I truly believe that there is in all of us a wish to succeed where all others have failed. I assume this is a normal component of the human animal. It has been my experience that teachers who stay in the field of education with emotionally disturbed children have a good deal of this quality within them. I also believe that this quality, when mobilized, frequently provides the ingredient necessary to achieve with these youngsters.

Finally, let me say that the normal child can adjust, adapt, and recover from poor or, let me say, less than adequate education. The emotionally disturbed child, because of deficiencies in his personality and ego development must have the best of all services available to him. What I have described is a good educational system that is essentially concerned with children and that takes into account all of the good mental health practices which are available to us.

AN INQUIRY INTO VARIATIONS OF TEACHER-CHILD COMMUNICATION: IMPLICATIONS FOR TREATMENT OF EMOTIONALLY ILL CHILDREN[1]

ROSALYN S. COHEN
RUTH LAVIETES
RENEE REENS
BIANCA RINDSBERG

Much has been written in the classics of world literature on the unending search of mankind for communication. Communication has at times been used interchangeably with love or even with humanness. Disturbances of communication are almost invariably considered part of all psychiatric illness.

"The psychiatric patient is often incommunicado — cut off from relatedness to others by his disorder and by the impaired understanding of him by his family and community. Not only is the psychiatric patient's communication with others seriously impaired; so also is his relatedness to himself — his intrapsychic communication. As part of therapeutic achievement, he is to be helped to communicate better with himself and with others; consequently, those in psychiatry and the allied professions require a particular sensitivity, skill, respect for communication between people and within themselves. Certainly the social and professional communities can better understand the psychiatric patient as they become more receptive to the possibility of communication with him, as they extend themselves in an inner listening (Spiegel, 1959, p. 909).

In the professional literature dealing with the treatment of mentally ill persons, the quality of communication has been referred to at times as a measure of pathology, a criterion for improvement or "cure," or even as the tool of therapy.

---

[1]This paper appears in these proceedings as an invited manuscript. All of the authors are affiliated with the Children's Day Treatment Center and School in New York City.

BACKGROUND OF PRESENT STUDY

In the broad spectrum of psychiatric illnesses of childhood, disturbed communication of parent to child has been postulated to bear a significant relationship to emotional disorder. To varying degrees, the impact of destructive (overhostile, overwhelming, detached, remote, rejecting or psychotic) parental communication is believed to be either causal or at least contributory to emotional disorder. What is less clear in the professional literature is what would constitute "therapeutic" communication in the treatment of these disorders, except that by implication it should perhaps be the opposite of what has been defined as "destructive" in the etiology of the illness.

The universal need of the child for communication with and from adults is taken for granted as an emotional prerequisite for the identification process by which he attains language, socialization, civilization and maturation. Few professionals today will contest the importance accorded to early family life and to parents as the arch communicators of values, emotional attitudes, standards for behavior and identification. However, the emotional impact on the young child of communication from the teacher as a first significant adult authority outside the home and family, as well as the spokesman for society, is a more elusive subject not as frequently explored in the literature of the behavioral sciences.

Need for Research on Teacher-Child Communication

It is a well-known observable fact that emotionally disturbed children, perhaps even more so than normal children, are particularly attuned to the feelings communicated by adults. They are frequently able to grasp the core meaning of a given message. This is quite a remarkable and fascinating phenomenon, considering that these children are besieged with more than average perceptual or environmentally determined distortions in the complex mechanism by which "normal" children sift meanings. By way of speculation, one might perhaps place this facility or hypersensitivity in the same class as the rather intriguing phenomenon of "psychotic insight."

In the early years of our Children's Treatment Center and School we frequently observed how quickly children picked up changes of mood, demeanor, tension level and/or other emotional communications by staff members, particularly their teachers with whom they were most involved by virtue of their six hours daily togetherness. Children with serious defects in other areas of reality testing often evidenced amazingly unimpaired emotional radar systems through which they picked up levels of feeling with lightning speed.

Bearing this special sensitivity of emotionally disturbed children in mind, and curious as to the nature and impact of teacher communication on the child and on the course of his rehabilitation, the staff of the Children's Treatment Center undertook the present study.

Description of Agency

This study represents a small beginning effort to inquire into the nature and emotional impact of teacher-child communication. It was undertaken in two classrooms of the Children's Day Treatment Center and School (Godmothers' League) of New York City from 1959 to 1962 (La Vietes, Hulse, & Blau, 1960).

The Children's Treatment Center was founded in 1956 to provide a three-year program of psychiatric treatment and special schooling for young children (age-range, 5½-9) who had been excluded from public schools because of the nature and severity of their emotional disturbance. The program was established in an effort to maintain these children at home and in the community, in preference to sending them to hospitals or residential centers. Its initial purpose was to attempt to rehabilitate these children so that they could return to public and/or community schools within three years through a three-fold service of: (1) psychiatric treatment of children; (2) special schooling under psychiatric supervision; (3) treatment of parents. Diagnoses covered a wide variety of emotional disorders including severe neuroses, behavior disorders and the childhood schizophrenias.

Children were placed into small classrooms of five children to a teacher. Teachers were carefully selected not only in terms of high professional standards of academic education, experience and training, but with a particular view towards the use of their personalities as an adjunctive therapeutic instrument in the overall treatment of the children. Treatment plans for each child were individually evolved by a team of psychiatrist, psychologist, social worker and teacher. Efforts were made to make maximum use of the child's school day to carry out such plans and achieve treatment goals. To this end the teacher was included in all professional planning and participated actively in making and carrying out therapeutic recommendations for the child and family. (LaVietes, 1962.)

Selection of Teachers for Observation

To undertake the present investigation, the authors decided to select two teachers in our special school in order to observe and analyze their communications to the child.

Both teachers were selected for these observations on the basis of their competence and skill. Both were considered to be highly successful in helping a series of children who presented severe behavior and learning problems in the classroom. Yet each teacher was a strikingly different type of person who worked in a style unique to herself. Each presented and used herself differently. Each used language and non-verbal communication differently.

In addition, each represented a different and distinctly opposite school of thought in terms of educational philosophy, teaching method, viewpoint as to role of teacher and proper functioning of a classroom for disturbed children. As a consequence, each had different expectations of the children and in turn evaluated her own success by different standards.

By virtue of these stark differences in personality, style, viewpoint, each teacher had created over the years a classroom atmosphere of such dramatic contrast that visitors were unanimously and immediately struck by this difference. The children who passed through their classes likewise experienced a different emotional climate with each teacher with resultant differences in overt behavior. Interestingly enough, differences in how well the children learned were not apparent.

Our curiosity was thus further aroused by how and why two different schools of educational thought, theories and methods, and particularly two divergent emotional communications, both produced apparently favorable "therapeutic" results with our children. Groups of children taught by these two teachers showed considerable improvement in school adaptation and functioning.

In an attempt to shed light on these differences, we set out to explore beneath their surfaces to seek answers to these questions:

1. How did the two classroom climates differ?
2. What and how did each teacher communicate to bring about such diffences in climate?
3. Were there any common elements which might account for their ultimate "therapeutic" success through two different paths?
4. How could their differences be maximally utilized to develop treatment plans to meet the needs of children with different emotional disorders?

Procedure of Investigation

To carry out this inquiry, a Research Committee was formed consisting of four staff members, one representative from each profession: child psychiatry, psychology, social work and teaching. The committee met and delegated a reporter to spend time as an observer in each of the two classrooms over a period of one year. Reporting assignments were rotated among various staff members who had special skills and sensitivities in observing and describing behavior. In addition, it was felt that such rotation would help to obtain more objective findings.

Each reporter spent fifteen minutes in each classroom on seven different occasions throughout the year, making a total of 14 observations. For purposes of attaining greater accuracy, two reporters were present at certain observations. On-the-spot process recordings were made of teacher-child interactions during these fifteen-minute observations. Efforts were made to include as many verbal and non-verbal interchanges as possible.

Following observations, typewritten transcripts were made and analyzed by the authors. Bearing in mind the limitations inherent in such process recordings, the authors set out to study and discuss the contents in terms of the significances of each teacher-child interaction. Style and content of the teacher's communication, verbal and non-verbal were likewise compared and analyzed.

Upon completion of all observations, each teacher was asked to make a personal statement of her idea of what she tried to communicate to the children in her class. The Committee then met to compare the subjective statements of intent with what had actually been observed and to draw some tentative conclusions.

We will attempt to present the results of this investigation in the following order:

1. A description of each classroom climate by one observer.
2. Analysis and comparison of levels of the teacher's emotional message, as obtained from transcript.
3. Subject statements by each teacher.
4. Common elements in message.
5. Differences and therapeutic implications.

Descriptions of two Classroom Climates

Classroom I — Miss C.

"In Miss C.'s class most of our children begin their three-year career at the Children's Treatment Center. They remain in this group for one year. In their initial period in this class the children are besieged with anxiety and fear of emotional contact. They cling to the periphery of the room, face the wall, hide in the bathroom or cower in a corner. Their eventual movement from the periphery to the center of the group is a long and slow process expedited by the teacher's special sensitivity to the emotional hunger, suffering and difficulties in identity and communication of these children. The sickest children are referred to this class, based on our assumption that here the child's bizarre ways will be accepted, his silences, incoherent or symbolic language and splintered communications understood, and his withdrawal, anxiety and disorganization best dealt with in the climate created by this teacher.

Miss C.'s voice is quiet and her manner unobtrusive, lending an air of relaxation to the classroom which is quickly communicated to the children. The quantity of talk is low, except for the soliloquizing of some children.

The pace of life seems slow to an observer until sudden explosions and lightning-like actions erupt. The child's dangerous actions do not evoke panic in this teacher. At these moments she moves quickly but without the haste and sharpness of motion which would betray a fear of not getting there on time. Imminent dangers are averted without the usual tension signs of an emergency, without anxiety or frustration reactions. Through repeated experience, the child begins to see in Miss C. an adult who is not afraid of his disorganization because she is able to render the harmful harmless.

The day's structure is upheld without pressure and strain. The children move toward and away from participation without disturbing this structure. The child's ways of participating and non-participating in group life are accepted. His wish to stay away or withdraw, as well as his wish to join are accepted without judgment. A child's retreat does not threaten the structure nor make him an outcast. There is no pull on his contribution but neither is he outside the day's plan. The teacher's way, the group's life are open for his inspection, for trial, to come into, to retreat from, or to participate in from a safe distance.

There is a work time, treat time, lunch time, gym time, visit the therapist time, and other times, but there is no time for *you do this for me*. The teacher requests no rewards for herself. The day progresses rhythmically; each part has meaning, closure and refrain. Each day the progression, in its essential form, is repeated. Thus, the routine of the day is known and exercised by the children and is not dependent on the teacher's will.

The child's performance is not judged — neither is the lack of it. Praise is expressed as a form of acceptance and acknowledgment of effort, but it is not a means that rewards the child's competence and by implication rejects that part of him which is not competent.

The teacher communicates her acceptance of the child and his deviations. His bizarre and primitive actions and utterances do not arouse anxiety or revulsion nor an academic type of tolerance. The teacher responds to the child's meaning or to his affect when his words fail to communicate. She responds to his message whether it is conveyed by silence, gesture or private language. Her implied message is: 'I know what you mean and in the common forms of thinking and saying this, it goes like so.'

Negativism finds little soil to root in. No counterweight is offered to balance the seesaw game of opposition. The teacher presents herself as an ally rather than adversary to the child. She is not in the main an authority to submit to or overthrow, a model to emulate or reject. She offers herself to the child as a source of emotional contact, nourishment and protection, ego preservation, and expansion.

The child's anxiety over personal adequacy finds little to feed on. Anxiety prompted by ego distintegration is mitigated by the teacher's awareness of the child's inner condition and her ability to supply the missing ego function — i.e., the control, support, or alternative the child cannot find for himself.

Children in this class are not confronted with the moral that good things come in limited numbers and must be parceled out in shares. Food and material supplies are abundant, but the communication that there is no scarcity transcends the actual size af the supply. The implication of unlimited supplies appears to be taken on faith by the child. There is virtually no hoarding, no competing for prized possessions, no rush and conflict to get more.

This extends to the teacher-child relationship. The child does not have to content himself with a 'share' of his teacher. Her attention, acceptance, and interest are not conveyed as measures extending in time with allotments for each. She is available to the child when he wants her. The time-honored principle of equal shares for everyone, by which parents defend against sibling rivalry seems here eliminated.

To sum up: The climate for living created by this teacher is not regulated by conventional standards for acceptance-rejection and is singularly free of the one-to-a-customer formula. In this climate the child's sickness is accepted, his disruptive and often primary process verbalizations are understood. The teacher gauges danger, confident that she will meet it in time to protect the child without manifesting the stress signs of an emergency. She communicates to the child her ability to protect him from his own destructive urges and those of others.

In this climate, which the children take in to varying degrees, fear is reduced, discouragement is relieved and the child may be able to rally his resources for growth."

Classroom II — Mrs. R.: Description of Classroom Climate

"Mrs. R.'s class is conducted along the lines of a traditional classroom. Conventional procedures provide the structure of a school day, oriented towards academic achievement and skills. Conventional rules for acceptable classroom behavior are taught and applied to a small group of children with an assortment of disturbances of learning, thought and affect. Children are encouraged to adopt patterns of behavior geared to group learning goals. The results appear to be effective.

Mrs. R. presents herself as a personality, a forceful presence with well-defined boundaries and social codes. Her person is carefully arranged and very pleasing to look at. Jewelry belongs to her presence. A pretty stone, a bright color, the clinking of charms on a bracelet become part of a child's view of her. Her appearance and total bearing are a clear statement about an ego that is separate. It is available for inspection and willing to serve as a social model, inviting and encouraging the child to do what she does, to do what she recommends.

The child's step in that direction, however small, is greatly encouraged and praised and there is constant readiness to acknowledge his dignity and worth, as well as his effort. There is recognition of the distance each child has to travel to reach the goal of social adaptation held before him.

To an observer the day progresses in an orderly fashion, along the lines of an achievement-oriented schoolroom. The program is well-balanced and geared toward a standard curriculum of skills and mastery. The children participate in varying amounts. Deviations of behavior, outbreaks of temper occur, but ruffle the calm only briefly. Infectious misbehavior spreads very little. Reverberations die quickly. Since there is no chaos or chronic disruption there is less cause for withdrawal and less contagious acting out. The children appear to be allied with the teacher and to share her goals. As a result there is more opportunity for learning academic skills, for engaging in peaceful and productive coexistence.

The climate is easy to be in. The teacher's hold is gentle, but persuasive and very firm. It withstands tugging, halts explosions, but permits quiet withdrawal in those who need it. It does not permit continued disruption by one child. Such a child is temporarily removed and casually readmitted, as if he had overcome an uncontrollable coughing fit. By her conviction that each child wants nothing more than to contribute to the group, the teacher is remarkably effective in obtaining participation. By aligning herself firmly with that fragment of the child's ego that is able to rise to her level, she is able to lead the child to adopt her goals and a view of life that is similar to hers.

She does not dwell on his pathology, but acknowledges its existence by humor. Mrs. R. 'kids' the child along with a kind of humorous intimacy in which she divests herself of the authority role and stands with and by him, becoming his friend. She chuckles at the human frailties expressed in his deviations, hoping he joins with her.

Thus she minimizes greatly the social onus of his pathology and offers him her faith that he can easily subdue it. 'Let's forget about it, let's get rid of it. Instead, let's work together on what is best for you. Follow my recipe and you'll do well.'

With this message Mrs. R. holds out the promised land of successful social adaptation to those who wish to reach it and she guides their faltering steps. In assuming that each child holds her goal she succeeds in some measure in implanting it. To varying degrees, the child in her class is motivated to suspend and submerge the symptoms of his pathology.

Thus the experience of many successful days in a productive atmosphere in which he has had his part, contributes toward the healing of the child's damaged self-esteem. It provides the child with practice in living normally within the required grooves of community schools."

ANALYSIS OF MULTIPLE LEVELS OF TEACHER COMMUNICATION

The variety of factors that weave together to form such vastly different emotional textures are difficult to separate and untangle. For communication is a complicated circuit, the net impact of which is greater than and different from each of its component parts.

Nevertheless, in order to simplify this task for purposes of discussion, we will examine and compare the different levels of each teacher's communication separately. To do this we will present some examples from each class which would most dramatically illustrate these differences in order to evaluate their significance.

"What I am like" (the person as message)

In his difficult and hazardous struggle for maturation the young child yearns for strong adults after whom to model himself. In his first encounter with the world outside the home, the emotionally disturbed child is particularly sensitive to the influence of the *person* of his first teacher.

> "Every person is a communicator; he plays various roles, with different and varying intensity; whether at various times or at the same time. Indeed, in some senses, the *person himself is the message"* (Spiegel, 1959, p. 911).

The successful teacher serves as a model and ego-ideal for every child. Children can often be seen to imitate her words and behavior and to incorporate her values. His need for the love and approval of the teacher (even if at first he sees her as an adversary and expresses this in negativistic or hostile acting out), provides the soil in which his eventual alliance with her may flourish. Only such an alliance can enable him to control his impulses and delay immediate gratification, both processes being necessary prerequisites for motivation of learning.

Let us examine these two teachers to see what they are like and how they present themselves to the child.

Miss C. presents herself rather neutrally. Her appearance seems to merge with the background. She wears a smock over her dress, walks silently on flat heels, and does not attempt to call attention to herself. Her voice is low and vocabulary simple. Her manner is quiet and unobtrusive. Her movements are slow and fluid, never sharp or abrupt.

She does not reveal her values and standards readily. They must be experienced by living with her. In so doing, one finds out that she is interested in the uniqueness and infinite variety of each child's personality. She is ready to meet him on his level and to use herself in whatever way necessary to help him. She is interested in whatever the child wishes to communicate. She communicates her acceptance of him and his bizarre behavior and deviation.

> Ira: "Why is Jeffrey waving his hands over his head?"
> Miss C.: "I guess he feels like doing that."

Without rejecting the child's unreality, Miss C. relieves him of its disorganizing effects by holding reality before him.

Miss C. is tacking children's drawings onto the bulletin board:

> Jeffrey: "Don't put a pin in my picture; it will hurt."
> Miss C.: "People hurt because they feel; pictures don't."

Mrs. R., on the other hand, presents herself more dramatically as an active, energetic, hardworking, cheerful, humorous, optimistic and tolerant person. Her appearance is enhanced by attractive bright-colored fashionable clothes which invite one to look at her. Her voice is forceful, her language colorful. Her presence, her personality is felt.

In her clothing, bearing, conduct, and manners she communicates her social propriety. By using herself as spokesman and advertisement, as model and salesman of our culture, she encourages the children to adopt her social values and behavior. She communicates that she knows how to get the best things from life, and that by imitating her they can do the same.

She believes there are greater rewards in submerging rather than expressing one's pathology. She offers these rewards in the form of lavish praise and oral supplies, whenever they do so.

> Mrs. R. has asked the class to respond aloud in unison. Linda, a child who does not talk at school, mouths the words silently.
>
> Mrs. R.: "Linda, when you speak up in a good, loud voice, I'm going to throw a party for the whole class. The works! Cake, candy, ice cream, favors, everything!"

To compare these two self-presentations, one might say that Miss C., through her neutral self-presentation invites the children to *use* her to supply deficient ego functions, while Mrs. R. through her persuasive and forceful outgoing self-presentation invites the children to *imitate* her.

"How I Deal With You" (the terms on which we communicate)

In her daily contact with children, the teacher is confronted with many alternative courses of action for dealing with behavior. When her choices are consistent, as they are in the successful teacher, they reflect an underlying point of view and value system. The premises of this system determine her choice of modality of communication. They serve as principles and set the terms on which she guides her communication with the child.

While Miss C. is in control of the classroom, her hold is not apparent. She sits around a table with the children. The children use her desk more than she does. She is often quite indirect in her communication. She never appears to be issuing directions but rather to be one of the group. The directives therefore appear to emanate from the atmosphere rather than from her. She verbalizes minimally, using her presence, movement, facial expression or a few words in interaction. She deals with the moment at hand — future goals are not mentioned. Physical contact is available to the child if he needs or desires it.

Her intellectual communications are the minimal needed for teaching. Information, facts, knowledge have no special value in her class. How people feel is given greater weight. She responds to what she believes the child is feeling or thinking rather than what he might be saying:

> Children are taking turns toasting marshmallows. Richard, a very fearful, autistic boy is extremely anxious to get his turn but too frightened of the other children to ask for it. He turns away from them and starts to chant subway station names.
>
> Richard: "IRT, 72nd Street, 96th Street, 110th Street."
>
> Miss C.: "I guess you'd like to get your marshmallow. It's your turn now."
>
> Richard faces the group, relaxes, and takes his marshmallow.

Here the teacher has allayed the anxiety behind the child's apparently irrelevant statements. She has responded to the feeling rather than the manifest content of his remarks.

Miss C. accepts the child's need to maintain a safe distance from the group and does not push for his participation.

> Neal, upon arriving, has crawled into his cubby and remained there. Teacher has made no move toward him beyond saying, "Good morning, Neal."
>
> After 20 minutes:
>
> Mitchell: "Why doesn't Neal come to the table?"
>
> Miss C.: "Neal likes to stay in his cubby in the morning until he gets used to us."

Here the teacher acknowledges the child's initial feeling of discomfort, accepts and interprets his way of dealing with it.

Mrs. R. adheres to social standards governing communication. She responds to what the child says rather than to its hidden content.

> Mrs. R. (teaching spelling): "Who can give me a three-syllable word?"
>
> Andrea: *"Troublesome* pest." (A hostile epithet used by the child's mother to her)
>
> Mrs. R.: "Troublesome, Excellent: *Trou-ble-some.* Three syllables. Very good, Andrea."

Here Mrs. R. accepts the response on its face value, disregarding its obvious emotional implications. However, by praising her for a good answer she makes Andrea feel better and in turn less "troublesome." By implication, she also communicates that *she* does not experience this child as "troublesome."

Mrs. R. encourages the child to participate in group life. She tries to create a group solidarity. *"We* are all wonderful." She urges him to conform to group standards.

> Charles: "I'm not going to sit down."
>
> Mrs. R.: "This is school and it is better if we all sit together to work."

She tries to inspire him to control his impulses in the service of long-range goals.

> Robert: "I'm going to kill Kirk."
>
> Mrs. R.: "No, you can control yourself and work on your reader so you can get a harder one soon."

In summary, each teacher sets different terms for the child to communicate with her. Miss C. responds to the emotion communicated by the child. Mrs. R. responds to the rational, logical and top level of his message. Miss C. does not press for the child's group participation. Mrs. R. tries to present the advantages of social participation. Each reassures and supports in a different way, by addressing herself to a different level of the child's need, communication and functioning.

"What You Can Expect From Me" (the structure and control I provide for you)

Whether underlying or apparent, a very successful classroom is based on a good deal of organization and structure. However, there is a wide range of variation in this structure contingent upon the ways in which the teacher exercises and conveys her authority, demonstrates her strength, maintains order and discipline. The predictability of the teacher, the use or absence of a punishment-reward system, the kind, quantity and quality of intervention and even the physical arrangement, all combine to give each classroom structure its special flavor. The way each teacher creates a group out of separate individuals has a time-table and a trademark of its own.

Miss C.'s classroom is arranged with large play areas, block and toy shelves on the side, and a large worktable in the center. Miss C. sits around this center table with her class, on a child-size chair. She stands only when moving to get or put away material. She does not use a blackboard. She does not address the group as such but moves from child to child, responding to each individually. She sometimes matter-of-factly comments on a child's special interests, preferences and fears.

"Allen likes arithmetic."
"Neal likes to be by himself sometimes."
"Roberta is afraid of the elevator."

Each child works at the same lesson in the sense that they begin together, but while arithmetic may be coloring a number for one, it may be adding a column of figures for another. Actual teaching is individual with Miss C. helping each child in turn while the others may work or dream or wander off temporarily. Unless children put themselves or others in real danger, their deviation is regarded in the same way as their conformity, as a reflection of their current level of functioning. While the difference between right and wrong is presented, ("2 and 2 make 4, not 3") there is no reward for good performance, no criticism for bad.

Linda: "I can tie it with a string."
Miss C.: "That's an idea. See if it works."

Levels of noise, tension, aggression, rise and fall without the teacher registering any reaction. An occasional statement ("That's not a good idea.") serves to intercept a child on the verge of some destructive activity. Only when danger is actually imminent does she rise and speak ("Throwing chairs is not allowed!") or move quickly to the side of the aggressor. Intervention is minimal and as brief as possible. When necessary, the child is held to prevent danger while an alternative suggestion is made calmly. Occasionally a child is sent out of the room when uncontrollable behavior mounts to a danger point and lengthy physical restraint would be required.

Mrs. R.'s class appears to be traditional except that she deals with five children instead of 30. The desks are arranged in rows facing the teacher's desk, which is at the front of the class. Behind her is a blackboard which is used to conduct most of the teaching.

Mrs. R. stands and addresses the group as a whole. She is the direct leader. She focuses the attention of the group around herself, while she enthusiastically presents the subject matter of the lesson. All the children are working on the same subject at the same time, although they are at disparate levels. She addresses questions to the group and selects a child to respond. She discourages diversions and abundantly praises appropriate responses.

Sometimes hand-raising is required. The children must contain themselves and wait their turn while she or others talk.

Mrs. R. makes it clear that this is what she expects. She spells out the rules for social behavior very clearly and leaves little room for doubt or misinterpretation. The rules are simple and clear-cut. They are reinforced by repetition and dramatization. They are posted on large charts and hung in front of the classroom.

"We talk in a quiet voice."
"We raise our hands before talking."
"We walk quietly in line."
"We do not run in the halls."

They serve as guidelines and limits for the child in controlling his impulses.

Those who fail to conform may be ignored, if they are not disturbing others. If they are, they are gently reminded, first by a look or gesture, then by an indirect comment: "I am waiting for all of us to settle down." If more forceful intervention seems necessary, physical proximity and a hand laid on the child's shoulder follows. The next step is a direct comment: "Andrea, turn around and look at the board." If none of this works, the child may be sent to another part of the room or warned that he must leave unless he ceases disturbing the group. This is the final step in the control process in which small infractions of behavior are made unacceptable — by inference, large ones impossible. ("We *never* push in this class.") It is a control process geared to the primary goal of group learning needs. To encourage the child to perform and conform she uses abundant praise:

Charles: "Can I use the stapler to do this?"
Mrs. R.: "Splendid idea; good thinking."

To encourage him to adopt the goals she has set for the group, she praises the group as a whole:

"This is the best *class* in solving problems."

"Now *we* are doing real hard grownup work."

In summary: Each teacher has a great deal of structure and control. In one group it is subtle and predominantly invisible. Miss C. relies heavily on hidden controls — prevention, physical arrangement, interpretation and her technique of not registering a moral reaction to minor misbehavior while reserving intervention for emergencies.

Mrs. R. relies more heavily on the forceful and clearcut presentation of structure and direct rules for social behavior, reinforced by constant repetition and active intervention.

"What I Expect From You" (standards of performance)

Through her receptivity to or rejection of certain productions or preoccupations of the child, the teacher communicates her expectations and standards of performance. Her use of competition, challenge, frustration, and gratification, are ways of telling the child what she expects from him.

Miss C. is primarily concerned with the child's feeling of safety and comfort in the classroom. She places no greater value on learning than on lunch or playing games. Each is viewed as equally important, valuable, and gratifying to the child. Her primary interest is in reducing the anxiety and discomfort that is part of his emotional illness.

Quality of performance is given no special merit. Therefore competition as an instrument of achieving performance is unnecessary and absent. Praise and criticism are equally absent. Lack of performance is accepted:

John: "Valerie doesn't know how to write the letters. She's tracing them."

Miss C.: "That's all right; that's how she does it now. Later on she'll write without tracing."

Challenges are minimal and not presented as such:

Miss C.: (to David) "Now you can turn to the next page."

David: "No, I'm not going to do any more."

Miss C.: "Okay."

Miss C. makes no effort to redirect or retranslate a child's communication into a curriculum instrument, but responds to it in terms of emotional need communicated by the child.

Scott: (while writing in workbook) "Jupiter is the biggest planet."

Miss C.: "That's right."

Neal: "How big am I?"

Miss C.: "You're as big as a seven-year-old boy."

Children are not required to accept frustration for its practice value. As much as possible, what the teacher provides is presented as gratifying. Delay and postponement in the service of exercise in self-control or long-range future goals and rewards are minimized, if not totally absent. Everything coming from the teacher seems gratifying. Frustration seems to arise only from the child's inner conflict or conflict with the environment outside the teacher. Power struggles with the teacher are rare.

Abundant supplies of food, candies, and gifts of small toys are always available, part of the day's routine, bearing no relationship to behavior, but designed to create a pleasurable atmosphere in which anxiety about deprivation, emotional hunger, inner tension, and conflict with others can be relieved, or at least diminished.

Mrs. R. values and expects learning and socialized behavior in the classroom. She praises and encourages the child when he progresses in these two areas. If he communicates his private preoccupations, feelings about himself or his family, etc., she does not respond, or suggests a diversion. She communicates to the child that in school it is better to forget such intrusions and turn to more interesting and rewarding activities.

She directs emotional communication into curriculum channels:

Joey: "I was very scared when I saw a lion in the circus."

Mrs. R.: "Maybe you can write a story about your trip to the circus."

Performance is highly valued. To achieve this, Mrs. R. presents the child with the degree of challenge which will require him to stretch and reach higher, but of which she feels him capable:

Linda: "I can't do this work."

Mrs. R.: "Yes you can. I know you can."

Since teaching is conducted as a class, each child becomes aware of his place on the performance scale. However, every effort to raise himself is enthusiastically applauded and admired.

Mrs. R. tries to balance frustrating activities (waiting turns, learning new skills) with gratifying activities (eating, receiving, motor releases, etc.) in accordance with her appraisal of the group's ability to accept a maximum of the former with a minimum of the latter. Her message is: "I expect you to accept frustration because it is necessary in living." Candies and gifts are distributed on holidays, birthday celebrations, and specific treat times each day to reward the group — for challenging performance, to take the edge off the less pleasant parts of the day and to encourage an overall pleasant atmosphere.

In summary: again we see that the climate of each classroom is colored by each teacher's communication of different expectations.

Miss C. expects that comfort will lead to greater school performance, while Mrs. R. expects the child to meet the challenges, competition, and frustration inherent in school learning, but tries to make these as pleasant as possible.

"How I Feel About Certain Things You Do"
(my value system and attitudes)

Each teacher brings into the classroom her own personal attitudes towards certain aspects of child life. These reflect her own special areas of personal investment, value system, philosophy of life and child rearing, moral convictions, and personal preferences. They tell the child how she reacts to the things he does and needs and demands.

MISS C.'s VALUE SYSTEM AND ATTITUDES

Value system. Miss C. introduces into her classroom some special and highly individualized attitudes towards conventional concepts of justice, equality, material things, possessions, cleanliness, and time, in an attempt to reduce the anxiety-provoking elements these concepts sometimes embody.

Attitude towards material and emotional supplies. Miss C. creates an atmosphere of plenty in her classroom. Supplies are always in abundance. "Just enough" is too little. There is always more to be had than anyone might require. She operates on the socialist principle — to each according to his needs. Since there is plenty for all there is no need to struggle with rivals for goods.

> Robert: "Wally is eating five crackers."
>
> Miss C.: "I guess he's hungry."

There in no differentiation between what the child wants and what he needs. With this as a working idea, the "equal-shares-for-all" concept of justice or "possessions-are-sacred" seems to disappear from the classroom.

She communicates to the children that *giving* (as opposed to withholding) is more enjoyable to her. This reduces the child's need to battle with her in order to extract what he needs or wishes.

Miss C.'s personal investment in material objects in the classroom is minimal. During activities she is not geared to preservation of materials or avoidance of waste.

> Scott: "I'm going to use all the paper."
>
> Miss C.: "There's plenty of paper in the world."

At the same time she is able to communicate that destruction is not permitted and there is curiously little material destruction in this classroom, considering the disorganization and varieties of acting-out behavior in these children.

She likewise sees no need to rush to do things in order to conserve or preserve time. She feels there is plenty of time in life for everything.

Miss C.: "In a few minutes it will be lunch time."

John: "I didn't finish my picture."

Miss C.: "That's all right, there's plenty of time to finish and then you can have lunch."

These attitudes and this leisurely pace seem most effective in reducing conflict and inducing peace.

Order. While Miss C.'s room is orderly in appearance, especially at the beginning of the day, it may take on a look of chaos during a messy activity. Miss C.'s investment is in the activity and she seems oblivious of the mess. She is casual towards dirt, spilling and messing, and accepts it as part of the child's living and doing. When an activity is completed she may then clean it up herself or quietly announce: "It's clean-up time," at which point the children may or may not join in helping.

Ira: "I spilled milk on the floor."

Miss C.: "That's all right, it won't hurt anyone. We can wipe it off later."

Conformity. Miss C. has an investment in the original and unique in each child. She values individuality and the children have considerable autonomy of expression within the boundaries of physical safety. Conformity for its adaptive value is not taught.

Ira: "David isn't working, he's running to the door."

Miss C.: "Yes, he likes to say hello to Mrs. Rindsberg."

She believes children will participate in and conform to group expectations when they have formed meaningful relationships with the teacher and children. By her awareness of interactions, timed interventions, she subtly engenders the group process. She interprets children's communications when their deviant ways of reaching out are likely to be misunderstood:

Mitchell, a silent child, tugs angrily at John's arm. John looks bewildered and turns pleadingly to teacher.

Miss C.: "John, Mitchell means he would like to play with you and be friends."

Aggression, regression, fantasy. Miss C. appears to pay little attention to impulsivity or aggression. Children often hit each other without her seeming to notice. She intervenes only at times of potential or real danger or in extremes of social defiance and material destruction, and then briefly.

Communications of regression are treated as part of the child's complexity of feelings and effort to deal with them. Only when they grossly intrude upon social structure are they discouraged.

> Gina: "I'm going to pee on the floor."
>
> Miss C.: "You do that in the bathroom."
>
> Gina starts to pull down her pants. Miss C. gets up and leads her toward the bathroom.

Miss C. responds to fantasy as to any other form of emotional communication. She comments on the fantasy with a view towards reassuring the child with the reality.

> Miss C.: "The letter C is like an open circle."
>
> Jeffrey: "I'm not supposed to close it. What will happen if I close it?"
>
> Miss C.: "If you do, we can fix it."

MRS. R.'s VALUE SYSTEM AND ATTITUDES

Value system. Mrs. R. on the other hand, adheres to generally held conventional concepts of justice and equality, equal shares to all of herself and of material goods.

Attitude towards material and emotional supplies. Mrs. R. believes that an individual's possessions are sacred. While she counsels not overreacting to breeches of this social rule, she respects it. She distributes supplies and uses time economically. She brings to the children's attention realistic limitations and cautions against waste and greed as socially undesirable.

> Irene: "Andrea is taking four chocolate bars!"
>
> Mrs. R.: "Let's each have one candy so that everybody will get a fair share."

Order. Mrs. R.'s class is orderly. If something drops she will pick it up immediately. As she moves about the room she will straighten a pile of books or put unused materials back into the cabinet. She feels that responsibility goes along with pleasure and that children should be taught the values of order and cleanliness. Dirt and disorder should be avoided and when they do occur remedied as fast as possible.

> Mitchell: "I made a mess with the paint."
>
> Mrs. R.: "If you wipe it up now our room will look nice and clean."

Conformity. Mrs. R. believes that it is necessary and valuable for a child to learn to conform, and she offers much gratification when he does so. She believes that conformity is both means and end for the child's social adaptation. At the same time she enjoys the child's individuality and flavor but guides it into the grooves of classroom structure. She herself is striking with her dramatic demeanor and high-flown language, always within social limits.

Aggression, regression, fantasy. Aggression and impulsivity are contrary to the dominant values of this class and are discouraged. Useful self-assertion and impulsivity and fantasy which can be redirected to make the school program more interesting are permitted.

> Robert: (starts to stand up and perform before the class)
> Mrs. R.: "If you come up to the front of the class we can have Show and Tell. You can show us the dance from "West Side Story.""

Withdrawal to one's inner preoccupations is considered undesirable but tolerable.

In summary, the world view, ethics and personal convictions of each teacher have entered into the kind of classroom she has created.

"How I let you know all of this" (style of communication)

While adult society stresses verbal messages as the primary means of communication, recent studies indicate that in certain life situations nonverbal messages have greater impact (Ruesch, Jurgen & Kees, 1956). In addition, the significance of a verbal message is influenced and its meaning sometimes altered by the person's style of speech, tone of voice, use of language, as well as accompanying gestures and body movements.

Throughout this presentation it is clear that each teacher has a significantly different style of communication.

Miss C. speaks minimally and relies heavily on indirect and nonverbal expression. She maintains frequent eye contact with the child. She sits most of the time and moves about quietly and inconspicuously. Everything about her conveys a picture of tranquility. When she speaks, her sentences are short, vocabulary well within the child's comprehension. She uses a *narrative* form in place of commands.

> The children are doing arithmetic and counting pencils one at a time.
> Miss C.: "Now Richard counts the pencils."

Mrs. R., on the other hand, is a highly verbal person. Her voice is strong and clear and she uses it to maintain contact. She talks to the children a great deal except when they are working quietly. Her vocabulary is colorful and spiced with uncommon words and foreign expressions. While the children may not understand the words, they get the meaning through the dramatic delivery and clearly conveyed context.

> Joey: "Here is my story."
> Mrs. R.: "Joey, that's the ultimate, the zenith, fabulous, the living end."
> Joey smiles, pleased.

Mrs. R. uses exaggeration, humor, large effusive motions and showmanship to hold the attention of the children. She tries to convince them that the world is wonderful and that there are many joyous feelings besides the feelings that disturb them.

Her facial expression is mobile and reactive. She moves about the room frequently and stands most of the time. She uses her body and hands actively. Her whole person conveys the idea of action. She works zealously to hold her audience. She enjoys and shows her enjoyment and excitement at the contents of learning.

In summary, Miss C. relies more heavily on the non-verbal while Mrs. R. relies more on the verbal. Miss C. is more the observer, and *reacts*, using herself as an instrument to encourage the children to communicate whereas Mrs. R. *acts*, using herself, her voice, her body as an instrument to convey her optimistic view of the world and to offer the child the possibility and advantages of adapting to it. Each communicates her own message in a style suited to its special flavor, and uses every facet of communication to make the delivery effective.

SUBJECTIVE STATEMENTS BY TEACHERS

After studying the different messages of these teachers, we then sought to find out what each teacher had *intended to communicate*, in order to evaluate the presence or absence of congruity between intent and finished product, as well as of a conscious design on their parts.

These are the written statements prepared by each teacher. They are presented verbatim to demonstrate what each teacher has in mind, and without the teacher's being aware of the objective conclusions about the observations.

Miss C.

"I can feel your anxiety and tension with yourself and others and will try to reduce these uneasy feelings in the classroom in all the ways I know how. I will be near you when you feel hurt, and/or lonely and give you privacy and distance when you need to be with yourself.

I try to understand your feelings and I can help you to understand that they are human. You can live with them and change them. I can help you to overcome their frightening consequences and to master them by my interpretations and reflections. I try to understand your communications, what you say, think, feel, communicate non-verbally or in disguised ways — so that I can better help you. I am aware of your difference and deeply appreciate that people are different because they have different feelings and have had different life experiences. I do not wish you to conform or to participate in group life until you communicate that you are ready to do so with comfort and pleasure.

Although I understand that you have angry and destructive feelings

I can control their consequences by the limits I set on your behavior. I can protect you by controlling your aggressive behavior towards others and theirs towards you.

You do not have to struggle with me or with other children to get what you need, for I am here to supply it, materially and otherwise. There is plenty of everything in the world and material things are for people to use and enjoy rather than to preserve and conserve. You do not need to rush on to the next activity as opposed to this one, for there is plenty of time in life for lingering on the way. Your care, problems, explosions, your need to touch me, to mess and make dirty do not burden or threaten me. Dirt is part of living and working and all children enjoy making it, and at some time perhaps eventually remedying it.

Through relaxed, predictable and pleasurable classroom living I aspire to help you to feel better about yourself and others, so that you will gradually feel more comfortable in the world and learn to master those things that are necessary to live in it."

Mrs. R.

"I am interested in your learning to perform in terms of curriculum and appropriate classroom behavior and to this end use my good will and skill as a teacher as well as my consideration of you. I know that you have troublesome feelings but these should be put aside so that we can perform our job together in the classroom. I think your attention should be focused on the teacher and the task at hand because this is the most productive situation for learning. I believe that children should participate and learn to conform for it is better and necessary for all social living to go along with the mainstream. You should learn to use materials constructively and appropriately. I realize that because of your illness you are disorganized and undirected, but I can help you by setting up an orderly classroom environment in which the day is well-patterned and broken up into units in accordance with curriculum and learning needs. I will see to it that your task will be made as pleasant as possible and in accordance with your abilities. I will help you to raise your level of performance. In adapting to my requirements you will find more satisfaction than in pursuing your own preoccupations, fears, anxieties or relations with other children. In trying to become like me, you will be following the right path for I am a good model for children. By following my leadership you will accept yourself more because you will experience success through tangible accomplishments. I encourage these accomplishments through my enthusiastic praise. You will soon feel more like other children, at least you will learn to behave as they do. Toward this end I will assist you as much as possible within the classroom structure."

WHAT ARE THE COMMON ELEMENTS IN THE MESSAGE?

We return now to our earlier observation that very sick children are tuned in to the underlying message communicated by the adult. Since the children seem to improve in both these climates, we were faced with this question: Was there anything in common, underlying these differences, to account for the favorable response to both? What did they have in common which led to this success and to which the children were essentially responding? What did they both communicate to the child that made him function better?

Common Content

We concluded from our observations that both teachers communicated a certain common content in both their messages.

Both enjoyed children, were kind and positive towards them, and communicated a sincere interest in and basic concern for the child as well as a wish and *ability* to be of help.

Both were conscientious and *well-organized*. This communicated strength, stability and effectiveness to the child.

Both were generous and able to give or feed the child although in different ways and on different levels; one in response to earlier emotional needs for feeding and maternal care, the other in response to the child's need for encouragement of mastery. Each communicated to the child her personal enjoyment of giving rather than withholding. "My giving to you does not go against the grain. I enjoy it."

Both avoided power struggles.

Both took the child's pathology in their stride. Neither panicked at it. One showed this by a kind of neutrality or non-registration of moral indignation, the other by de-emphasizing it with the child and helping him to forget about it.

Common Form — How They Said It

Consistency. Each teacher showed great consistency and congruity between intent and performance (deed) in her communication. In comparing each teacher's statement of intent with her classroom climate, the two fit together. The message intended is the message carried out. "I do what I believe."

Each teacher showed great consistency between her verbal and non-verbal communications. Her movements, expressions, gestures, did not say the opposite of her spoken words. The message stood intact, without contradiction. The words stood behind the behavior and the behavior stood behind the words. The levels of communication reenforced each other. Thus the child received one consistent message from the teacher. The message rings true.

The total personality of each teacher matched and enhanced her intended and actual communication. The person and the message were of one piece.

Conviction. Each teacher had great conviction about what she was doing, her philosophy and design. "I believe strongly in what I am doing."

Style. Each teacher communicated her point of view in a style well suited to the most effective delivery of her message. The style of communication reenforced the content. "My way of saying things fits what I say."

SOME CLINICAL IMPLICATIONS

In looking over these common features, we were especially struck by the therapeutic value of a consistent message to the emotionally disturbed child.

Double Bind Message

Much has been written in the psychiatric literature about the disturbing effects upon a child of the "double bind" or dual message (Bateson, Jackson, Haley, and Weakland, 1956). Bateson's double bind hypothesis refers to incongruities between feelings and behavior, resulting in a dual message. The dual message takes many forms. A movement can contradict the verbal statement. For example, the adult says to the child, "It's time to go now," and stands still herself, indicating that she has no expectation that the child will carry out her instructions.

Parental Perplexity

William Goldfarb has referred to parental perplexity as both responsive and contributory to the difficulties of schizophrenic children (Goldfarb, 1958).

Indecisive movements convey to the child, "I don't understand my own feelings in this matter or in relation to you," or "I don't know which way to move or what to do." Unsolved conflicts in the teacher can result in movements or gestures which contradict the spoken word. For example, movements can convey anxiety while the adult speaks words of reassurance. "Everything will be all right," may be stated with a quivering hand and accompanying perspiration which both convey the adult's anxiety and contribute further to the child's anxiety. Not only

94

are such messages confusing to the child, but often the child responds to the non-verbal or latent message that is conveyed through movements.

Thus, we have found that one single clear-cut message to the child, in and of itself, has therapeutic value (provided, of course, that the overall intent and message are essentially benign and well-meaning). It communicates strength, clarity of thought and feeling as well as the ability to be of help.

In addition, we have found that verbal and non-verbal communication serve different therapeutic aims in the education and treatment of the child.

Therapeutic Use of Class Placement

Although one cannot mechanically recommend the therapeutic matching of one diagnostic category of illness with either type of teacher, we have formulated some tentative recommendations for class placement. They are based on a determination of the needs of the child in terms of:

(1) Time-table of child's illness and therapeutic course. For example: A child at the beginning of treatment might do best in the climate of Miss C. geared to earlier emotional and developmental needs, while a child at the end of treatment might need the climate of Mrs. R. geared to higher maturational goals.

(2) Factors of family dynamics. Deviant mothering of one type or another might require that the child experience one type of teaching or the other to help undo pathological results. A psychiatric evaluation of the specific noxious family influence causing or perpetuating the child's illness would help to determine the therapeutic milieu which might best undo these influences.

(3) Nature and dynamics of child's illness. The classroom climate of choice is partially determined by the dynamics and nature of the child's illness. One type of schizophrenic illness might need one kind of structure, another a different type of structure.

Since it is apparent that one teacher (Miss C.) works from the inside out, the other (Mrs. R.) from the outside in, we will next examine what types of children would derive the greatest benefit from each.

Children who have been exposed to excessive verbiage and intellectualization by parents, respond more favorably to a teacher style that is predominantly non-verbal (Miss C.). Children who have experienced parental verbalization as a barrier to emotional contact, respond better to non-verbal style. This is also true of children who experience talking itself as a direct attack.

Verbal communication, on the other hand, provides the child with an opportunity for direct confrontation which can be used for insight and interpretation in the treatment. Clear verbal communication can help psychotic children to minimize confusion and clarify perceptions (Myers & Goldfarb in press. In addition, the child who has experienced parental hostility and rejection through silence would obviously respond better to emotional contact maintained through talking. The verbal mode of communication is used primarily in the classroom of Mrs. R.

In addition, we will present other therapeutic values of each classroom environment.

Therapeutic Values of Classroom I (Miss C.)

We have found that this classroom atmosphere is of greatest value to these types of children.

1. The child who has suffered maternal deprivation; angry, orally deprived and affect hungry children flourish in this climate of abundance and feeding. Children who need to experience fulfillment of earlier levels of dependency and need for closeness seem to thrive in a warm cuddling classroom environment of nurturance and gratification.

2. Children of over-repressive parents who have been "locked in." Repressed children who need opening, unfolding, unlocking the dam to permit release of feelings, do well in Miss C.'s class. If emotional channels are available in the child and in the environment to change feelings and attitudes, this channel serves to help organize rather than disorganize the child. Opportunity is provided for reflection and mastery of feelings.

3. Children who have been "locked out" by over-narcissistic or intellectual, remote, detached or emotionally sterile parents; such children need an environment conducive to expression of feelings, an opportunity for emotional contact and emotional airing.

4. Children who have experienced overwhelming or overbearing parents and as a result have become detached or withdrawn; they need some initial distance to permit them to pace their safe movements towards human contact. They need a delicately paced emotional approach that allows for emotional experimentation. The withdrawn, quiet, fragile child who needs less intrusion responds to more gentle, individualized and non-directive handling.

5. Children who need to learn to make contact with other children; they need less external structure in an atmosphere that permits them to find their own comfortable ways of communicating with other children and working through relationships.

96

6. Children who require closeness and mothering divested of emotional and performance demands; depressed children who need to experience unqualified acceptance and love for themselves rather than for what they produce to enhance parents. Such children need a classroom in which they can be accepted without having to produce.

7. Children whose illness is such that they need minimal pressure and stimulation. Highly fearful, anxious and panicky children who need relaxation of structure improve in this type of classroom.

8. Passive-aggressive children who have experienced severe power struggles with adults and have acquired subtle weapons for battling and overpowering the adult in turn. They remain fixed in the early stages of non-conformity. The adult is bound to lose the struggle. Such children need an atmosphere divested of you versus me elements, but which allows for expansion of the child's autonomy and opportunity for some non-conformity. Such children turn all demands and expectations into occasions for struggle and need to have these relaxed for this reason.

9. Very slow or very bright disturbed children who need to learn to relate by means other than achievement show considerable improvement in this classroom.

10. Paranoid children who completely distrust adult intentions need minimal overt interference to allow for a period in which they can observe the adult and evaluate his motives.

11. Self-punitive children who defeat adults by harming themselves — need to be in an enviroment where there is no punishment — reward system of any kind.

12. Children with severe sibling rivalry problems who feel that somebody else's gain is their loss do better in a non-competitive environment where gratification is available to all without conventional measurements.

13. Children with identity and body image problems — as they have no sense of self they need an approach that provides special didactic methods for teaching identification, accompanied by techniques of handling geared to their uniqueness. Such children need a classroom in which discussion includes reflection on the impact of their personalities on others.

Therapeutic Values of Classroom II (Mrs. R.)

In the well-structured conventional classroom guided by the clearcut teacher model who clearly spells out rules for social behavior, we have found these types of children do best:

1. Certain ego-fragmented children who have failed to respond to treatment geared to inner feeling changes. They remain hollow inside

and need a climate in which they can at least learn how to feel and behave through imitation, rote learning and signposts with social cues. They need a plastering job to help them make at least a surface adaptation (the "as if" child). Since their state of disorganization has been inaccessible to other forms of help, and since further expression of fantasy and pathology serves no therapeutic end, they need to have their pathology repressed. They do better when given a set of comeback rules which they can learn by rote and imitate. In the clearly rule-run environment, they are able to pick up those cues which help them to form at least an outer skin of adequacy. They are taught what is expected clearly and learn to simulate appropriate behavior. Since the flooding of their thoughts and fantasies serves only to further deteriorate or destroy them, they need to have the dam closed or stopped up. Repression and tightening is the treatment of choice.

2. Some children's social responses are so flattened that they need a graphic poster-style presentation of society in order to grasp its cues. Reality must be carefully spelled out for them in detail and with constant external reenforcement. Some children don't feel anything and may never. They need intellectual substitutes for feelings. They need active intervention which provides alternative activities for each minute and pulls them up by the bootstraps of their ego function.

3. Certain schizophrenic children who live in constant fear of their fantasies of disintegration and whose disorganization is so all-consuming can only function in an atmosphere which by its very order and rigidity offers them a more comfortable and secure substitute for what they are thinking about. It gives them a minute-to-minute schedule for living. It rescues them from their dreaded fantasies by substituting a planned program which permits expression only in areas of academic interest. This is anxiety reducing for such children.

4. Children of parents who, for whatever reasons, do not provide social models for the child, benefit in this class in which clearcut models and simple cues for behavior are carefully spelled out. Such a climate offers the child a substitute for a deficient family structure.

5. Some children who fear the invasion of intimacy find greater comfort and reassurance when a cloak of anonymity is provided for them. In the group-oriented "togetherness" and "we" atmosphere they are pulled into the stream of things. This brings the deviant child into the family of man. His successful participation in such a group in turn enhances his ego and self-esteem.

6. Children whose distrust of the adult has diminished to the extent that they can now make a connection, are ready to perceive what the

adult wants and to adapt to the environment. They now have some capacity for identification with outside, some stake in conformity. They have reached the stage where they want to be like others and are ready for the incorporation of and direction from the adult.

7. For some children the teaching of skills is the best route towards greater self-esteem. Children who by virtue of emotional maturation, therapeutic intervention, readiness or intellectual brightness are ready to give up immediate gratification and substitute intellectual challenge, need increased demands and expectations and are ready to accept and use pressure. They can be convinced or mobilized to deliver. Channels for intellectual contact are now available within them and they look forward to achievement. This achievement can, in turn, enhance their self-image.

8. Children who have been overinfantilized and encouraged to remain at an immature level of adaptation — they need to have pressure introduced with reasonable expectations for mastery. They need to have the adult's emotional investment in his mastery and achievement rather than on his fixation at an earlier level.

9. Children who receive unconscious parental messages to act out; children whose parents for various reasons are unable to set limits or control behavior which may result in the child's feeling omnipotent — such children need strong external help in controlling impulses which they have not as yet experienced from an adult. They need firm control and encouragement towards repression.

10. Children who get or perceive unclear or distorted messages from parents on how to behave — need clear spelling out of the impartial message, "This is how to behave. I don't want you to do singular things."

SUMMARY AND TENTATIVE CONCLUSIONS

The concept of combined day treatment and special schooling evolved as part of the need to find new and better ways of helping emotionally ill children. It is part of an ongoing search and research for greater understanding of the needs of different types of childhood illness and the most effective tools for treatment.

Successful school adaptation is an inseparable part of the rehabilitation of the disturbed child. The 30 hours weekly that the child spends with his teacher can serve as a vital adjunctive tool for achieving therapeutic goals. It can extend "treatment time" over a full week. The classroom can provide the child with a life situation in which he can test and expand his resources and therapeutic gains. It can provide him with an emotional climate for living which can offset the pathological influences in his life and thereby serve to counteract his illness.

The present study was undertaken to attempt to clarify the type of emotional experience the classroom can provide which can best dovetail treatment goals. Two teachers were selected for observation who were viewed as most therapeutically effective by our clinical staff. An analysis was made of the kind of emotional climate each had created in his classroom, and the multiple levels of communication through which such a climate was achieved.

Since the two teachers worked so differently, we set out to find out whether, underlying these apparent differences, there were in fact any similarities in their communication which might conceivably account for their common success. We concluded that there were such similarities which accounted for their common effectiveness. These characteristics are outlined and suggested to be necessary for all persons in those professions engaged in treating disturbed children. They are briefly, acceptance of and concern for the child, a wish to help him towards health plus the organization and consistency to communicate these effectively.

In exploring their differences we concluded that each created a type of life situation which performed a different therapeutic function for the child. By careful selection and placement of children whose treatment goals could best be achieved or realized by each, we could make maximal use of their differences.

IN SUMMARY

Since communication is the tool of teaching as well as therapy, a greater understanding of the communicative processes involved in adult-child relations would help to refine techniques of treatment as well as education. An attempt has been made and described to explore varieties of communication in two teachers who participated successfully in a day treatment program. Therapeutic uses of their similarities and differences were suggested.

Perhaps future reseach designs might evolve methods for detecting children's responses and getting their view of what adults are actually communicating. In the meantime, we hope we have made at least a beginning inquiry into the ever-fascinating subject of what it is we are all really telling each other.

REFERENCES

Bateson, G., Jackson, D.D., Haley, J., and Weakland, J. Toward a theory of schizophrenia. *Behav. Sci.*, 1956, *1* (4), 251-264.

Goldfarb, W. Parental perplexity and childhood confusion. In A. Esman (Ed.), *New frontiers in child guidance.* New York: International Universities Press, 1958.

LaVietes, R. The teacher's role in the education of the emotionally disturbed child. *Amer. J. Orthopsychiat.*, 1962, *32* (5), 854-862.

LaVietes, R., Hulse, W. C., and Blau, A. A psychiatric day treatment center and school for children and their parents. *Amer. J. Orthopsychiat.*, 1960, *30* (3), 468.

Myers, D. and Goldfarb, W. A study of parental perplexity in families of schizophrenic and normal children. *Amer. J. Orthopsychiat.*, in Press.

Ruesch, J. and Kees, W. *Nonverbal communication,* Berkley and Los Angeles, California: University of California Press, 1956.

Spiegel, R. Specific problems of communication in psychiatric conditions. In S. Arieti (Ed.), *American Handbook of Psychiatry.* New York: Basic Books, 1959, 909.

SUMMARY DISCUSSION

WILLIAM C. MORSE

This final report will not be an organized coverage of the many things which have happened in these two days. Nor will I try to name the contributors of the portions which serve as the basis of these reflections. I hope these remarks will not just be repetitious of what has transpired but rather the coordination of issues which were stated or implied.

It will take me a very long time to digest these two days. I'm certain many of you feel bottled up with things that have occurred to you which there was no opportunity to express to others. However, I have listened to some of the talk between sessions and parts of this will be incorporated as we go along.

One of the problems in the Conference stems from the variety of people here and the various roles represented. We range from program starter people and supporting personnel to the immediate conductors of the classroom action. There are people with big programs, with little programs, with public school classes and institutional programs; sometimes we talk across each other because of the contrasts in focus. Nevertheless, it was interesting for me to hear in your between-session talk how much each one of you learned in your own way and from parts of the program which I might not have anticipated. Helpful ideas came from different places for different ones of us. All have been caught up in the spirit of the Conference, encouraged by the interest expressed and stimulated by the fact that so many stayed through these two days of an intense experience.

One of the things worth recognizing is a real ambivalence that plagues us all. There is the matter of understanding the basic issue and putting what we're doing into a total context including trying to comprehend it on the one hand and solving the many immediate, irritating issues of the present moment on the other hand. We went back and forth between these two poles. When you have a specific issue it makes you uneasy not to get an answer. When you are confronted with a big issue that causes you to think about reformulation of an overall sort this is

---

1. This discussion was recorded at the Conference for presentation in these proceedings.

another level. Both have been of deep concern here and one seldom sees a Conference with this back-and-forth as prominent as it has been here. As a profession, all of us ought to be involved in both solving the problem of an immediate pupil in a particular class as well as the broad spectrum.

Now, we did start a quest for uniqueness which was emphasized this afternoon particularly. We learned that each of us in our own area must work out a program with a unique design. We haven't talked about the individual variants ranging from protected classes to programs in junior high with tandem teachers. There are many other ways of doing things and we have looked at only a few. Another Conference might well address itself to the ways of actual variant designs for some of these things. Further it is not classes alone, but it is the articulation of these classes and the coordination with other programs in the school and community. In our own state study of needs for disturbed children, the agencies all say that for 50% of the youngsters which they are asked to serve, they cannot provide the necessary treatment or help. They are the "wrong kids" for their service. We must recognize too that, no matter what we do along the way, we will have to provide for those children who cannot be allowed to roam free in the community because of what they might do to themselves or others. It would not be humane to permit them freedom. They make up in intensity what they lack in numbers. Especially at adolescence whose serious difficulties foul up programs which are not adequate for them from the beginning to the end. So whatever we do about non-institutional programs I hope we also make provisions for the minority of very disturbed children who should be institutionalized. In other words, there are children who cannot use an open setting and putting them there is contraindicated.

Now there is another thing that we haven't talked enough about in this connection. It is the *calibre* of the program which makes the difference, not just having a program. The problem was raised in connection with training personnel and this is going to plague us because we really need a high level of proficiency. It isn't just a matter of having more classes or more programs because if they're no better than some other things we have done in the past it would be better not to start any more. We must be certain that what we do we do well all the way through. This is in the face of the fact that there's already a scarcity of personnel and it was pointed out this scarcity will increase in the years ahead.

Another matter which permeated the Conference was the almost desperate effort to conceptualize our processes and our problems. In particular there was an astute recognition that what we do is part of the total social fabric. I'm sure that we generally avoid this because it is such a depressing thing to think of the whole social order in its complexity. However, without this recognition what we do is merely an island without attachments. We learned much about social processes and we learned that they are not random. There is an interplay of overall forces with any specific problem we face. It was pointed out our task is not just to appreciate this recoil sequence but to sense the manifestation in our own locale and develop the program we need to utilize the forces. I think our problem is how not to be a captive of these social processes which we recognize are taking place. Our future depends upon how we control them in this unstable decade ahead. It is like a developing weather front and the question is, how can we react to it rather than just being overwhelmed or controlled by it. This is a matter of anticipatory monitoring. As we learn to look at the total stimulus pattern in our communities we get to understand why some programs develop rapidly and why certain programs plateau and even decay. It may really be that they are riding a crest of one of these waves we heard about. And sometimes we forget that we're going to pay a price for rapid development when the wave passes on.

I think our problem is how to get reasonable sustained efforts to deal with what we know are the chronic problems which will not be solved by crash efforts. We represent the decision makers and the doers. How can we use these community social cycles effectively to help stable, long-term programs? We learned about the visible aspects of threat and recoil but I would say we have yet another problem — the tolerated and submerged problems which are there, too. These are the big problems which we somehow come to tolerate. Maybe this is one of our difficulties. The problems of human rights, of segregation, of poverty and of housing were commented upon. These are submerged aspects of delinquent manifestations which produce threat and recoil. Often we don't think about the submerged conditions which are a cancer. The usefulness of the one healthy thing we do is eaten away. The question in my mind is, "Will we have the follow through to really do more than just a little fine job that we think about accomplishing?"

We talked about the home but we skirted the implications, our experiences. There must be new ways to work with homes. Some communities have point systems, and they serve only the children who have so many points. A child gets points if the father will come to therapy. Other agencies are willing to work with the great unwashed where parents won't come in for what we euphemistically call "help." It has been our experience sometimes that you're better off not working with parents when the child is the scapegoat of the family situation. The less you do with certain parents the better the child's chance of survival. We ought to reexamine this whole process which we didn't really get into but there were those who asked questions. This is a topic for some intensive thinking of new concepts in working with parents.

We also have the question of program extensiveness, moving out from the classroom into the community. Are we going to go as far as finding jobs for adolescents? Or are we going to have our nice little place of business which is perfect because we have all disciplines hovering around but the program doesn't go anyplace? I have a concrete suggestion to make to those who really believe what we were told about the social process. Demand equal cash and equal investment for prevention for every investment in correction. Every dollar for correction matched with a dollar for prevention or we won't pay. I wonder if we have the guts to do that. We could say we will have one class if they will provide one helping person to prevent us from needing another class next year. Are we going to have quid pro-quo, person for person, so when you put a teacher in the special classroom you put a helping person in for prevention? If we won't sell out for less, then I think we really registered the message we heard this morning about the nature of the design of community action. It is so much easier to do the little specific things. We can have a good program as a defense against really doing anything about the big issue. We do our project and feel so good about it. In our Council for Exceptional Children study we found this to be true. Personnel would brag about one class in the midst of debris. Now, if we're really professional and if we got the message, we will say, "O. K. Match prevention and restorative efforts."

Another issue came which seemed important but we didn't examine it too closely. Perhaps this is because it still hasn't gone far enough. I refer to the implied symbiotic relationship between the disturbed, the deprived, and part of the retarded and some of the underachievers. They are being amalgamated from the way we talk. It is too new to cause defensiveness yet but sooner or later we will tred on some toes. We will be invading private domains when these are brought together. We can still talk about this as a theoretical matter. I'm sure certain ones will say, "Well, they can't do that, they don't know about this kind of a kid" or "They don't know about that kind of a kid" as we really begin to draw these four areas closer together. If we do bring these things into some symbiotic relationship I hope we take the *best* of the three or four methods and not the worst of each. Will we really get the essence of each of the techniques from these various fields to bring to bear on this new combination? We heard the suggestion that it be called "supplemental" education vs. categories upon categories. If you took even these four or five types of children and considered all the possible permutations there might be — a pupil with a little under-achievement, a bit of emotional disturbance and a dash of deprivation. There are endless combinations. The idea was, we ought to think of these fields in a more unified way but we will need an approach which focuses on a child and not a type.

Back of the type theory is a concept that once you get children of a type together they are homogeneous. I think this is the number one illusion of Special Education — when you separate them out you have a homogeneous group and thus you can deal with them in some unified fashion. The individual differences in these so called homogeneous groups which we assemble are even greater than those in the regular classroom. Of course the special teachers know that. Because there are fewer of them in a room or because they are labelled in one way we act as if they are more alike. I think what we have really been talking about is the fact of multiple handicaps in new patterns and new arrangements. We have an awareness of new designs of problems from those that we accepted before. Let's not waste our time in making all new labels. Now I hope we won't have a threat-recoil cycle as we put these together and say that they're all alike when we know that no two of them are alike no matter what kind of combinations they are. So, it worries me a little bit that as we amalgamate, the illusion of homogeneity will be in the background and we will be caught again. We'll be treating the symptoms as if underachievement in the retarded child is the same as in a de-prived child, is the same as in a disturbed child. I hear more and more talk this way these days and I wonder if really you're willing to settle for that. Within the supplemental design there is really a school for each child which he is going to create anyway. So the question is, "Can we create a unique school design?" Let me give you an example from a discussion about high school disturbed children. They were going to design *a* program but when we looked at them we found at least three major sub-categories in addition to all the individual ones. There were certain school alienated children: no matter what you did you could never win them over to the glory of education but you could provide for them, through a work experience, a chance to begin to participate in the culture.

The second group were school failures. They wanted desperately to belong although they wouldn't always admit it at first. If there was any-thing they could do to join the middle-class race they would join. But they weren't achieving very well and were having trouble. They needed much support and remedial help. Third, there were some very sick adolescents in this group, though still in high school. No program that a high school could provide would do more than mediate their difficulties enough to help them exist in that environment. Now, within these three patterns there were many sub-patterns. We cannot forego looking at the real nature of our clientele.

Still another issue came up which we never faced very squarely and this one happens to be most irritating to me. I'm about to foist my irritations on you. This is the class difference stereotype. We fooled around with this and played footsy with it but we didn't face it. I'm frankly tired of the middle-class being the scapegoat of our society. It is time that we examine this notion. I wonder if there are not basic human values which supersede class values which always seem to be interposed. I hope you have read *Compulsory Miseducation* by Paul Goodman. If you haven't, I would suggest you read at least the section dealing with values. It may irritate you too much to read the whole thing, but read the part on class-values. This content was hinted at by one of the speakers from the audience. While there are lower-class values, middle-class values, and upper-class values, there are also HUMAN values. What are these? And are these not the ones to which we should be sensitive? I think we have put up a screen with this middle-class value business in order to distort. It isn't middle-class values, it's poor socialization in the human being that we're dealing with. We label it middle class because somehow it is popular today to flagellate ourselves. I don't understand that phenomenon, but I can see the practice. These human values include the ability to establish relationships with people, which seems to me classless. Is the aim of a higher realization for all of our people a class value only? There are values of western civilization. You can damn them for that if you want to (thereby expressing other implied values), but it seems to me someplace we must have standards and this is no cause for shame. Our experience with teachers who come from the "terrible" middle-class is that some of them are just as good teachers in rough areas as are others from the lower-class. As a matter of fact, some from the lower-class are not very effective teaching in the areas where they originated. They have more problems than the strangers if they are strangers to human beings. Do I have to be schizophrenic to work with the schizophrenic? Let us abandon this notion. We ought to look to the personal qualities of the people who wish to teach rather than to what class they came from. The correlations of behavior and class are lower power at best and no power applied to an individual. It has been our experience that there are wonderfully empathic persons from any class who can learn to teach children of various classes effectively. I think we skirted this at the Conference.

We heard these two days much about the deprived. We have created a new minority group, "deprived" and they are fast becoming a stereotype. If a pupil is "deprived" and he sits there "we can tell you something about him." Actually one can tell practically nothing about him by labelling him deprived. In our own study of deprived school children we found at least five different aspects of deprivation which break down the stereotyped. One of them is economic. There are hungry children in our schools every day — and it is very hard to teach a hungry one. Maybe what they need is to be fed, and not with some psychological food stuff either. Real bread might help.

Then there are those who are deprived of the necessary educational precursors. They have been denied the experiences which get them ready for school. Others are deprived of emotional relationships á la Spitz. And we have found still others, particularly boys, deprived of models. They have no reasonable person to emulate. There are also those that are deprived of hope — who have no belief in their future. The joke of life is over early. Even in the first grade you know you won't be president. Now these several types of deprivation tend to be class-related but they are not necessarily class-saturated. This is quite different. Although the economic deprivation and lack of educational precursors will be more frequent in lower-class children, the emotional relationships of children in any class may leave them deprived. Many lower-class children have had better mothering than some of us have had. Let us not distort the reality by labels. In any block, slum or suburb, there are many different types of children. I'm upset about this deprivation term and how we're using it. I would also suggest to you that if Freud is right for one class he is also right for other classes. He studied human beings. But a lot of times we have one psychology for one class and a different one for another as was several times implied in this Conference. In my clinical experience, if you don't have a father or know who he is, it doesn't matter what class you are in. It hurts your identification. And this is what Freud taught us.

In a study our group at Michigan did, it was found that the aggression of the middle-class and lower-class was not different in amount but rather different in nature. The middle-class does the needling and the lower-class does the swearing, but the amount of torture inflicted on another human being by aggressive behavior was not established by class. These are things, I think, which make us wonder about the simplified, popular thinking about class. If we are to a large degree an homogenized culture born of mass media, had we not better be very careful about how we ascribe class differences to people? Some programs are already producing backfires by this kind of labelling.

Another area which came up from time to time was "What is special about Special Education?" It was mentioned in a dozen different ways. The basic issue, as we were helped to see by one of the papers, depends upon what teaching is in regular education. The definition given indicated that "it depends upon an articulated set of concepts useful in handling the array of problems faced by the classroom teacher." We learned that regular education does not yet have this articulated set of concepts. We certainly do not have the concepts when it comes to special teaching. There is much clarification yet needed in conceptualizing regular education, the parent of Special Education. These two jobs can be done in tandem. We can't wait until there is agreement on what regular teaching is before we get to work on what we're doing, but the two will be interlaced. Much can be done through action research in the setting, as we saw demonstrated in the Conference. And to get an action researcher in the setting will take double courage: first on the part of the researchers to go where real life exists that defies control, second on the part of those who are teaching to let these "snoopers" in and trust them and work with them. We had a tremendous demonstration of the possibilities in one of the papers.

Perhaps every college which gets a grant to train teachers ought also to have a liaison with an ongoing program in one of the public schools or institutions so that there is a joint relationship and research. They are now so far apart that we have to build bridges to connect them. It will take honesty to discover what is special about Special Education.

During this Conference we heard that there are mutually contradicting cliches about teaching. One area of cliche is the role of authority in teaching. We heard that the meaning of most of the generalizations about teaching, and I think this means special as well as regular, disintegrates upon examination. That may be why we usually hesitate to examine them. If even the cliches are in conflict, what is left? Tone? Procedures? When does humor leave banter to become sarcasm? And how does one tell? We want to know some of these things and it's obvious that we have a lot of work to do in this connection. In our Conference report the need to work at two research levels at once was closely outlined. We must work both toward defining the specific and the precise as well as the general pattern in which the specific action exists. We heard that teachers make decisions — hundreds of them every day—and I think this is what makes teachers tired by the time the closing bell sounds. We heard that it would be a good thing if we teachers could understand our "druthers" more completely, which is one way of understanding ourselves. We heard about the consequences of strain in selecting the best of the various bad decisions at your disposal. I think this is the most fatiguing of all — to make the least terrible of all the possible terrible decisions. And we heard from several people that part of the problem is not what teachers *want* to do but what teachers are *required* to do by the set of circumstances. Another major contribution to our understanding is the evidence that there are many ways, or many patterns of effective teaching so far as we now know. To a degree, then, each is not to initiate a pattern that someone preordains but to evolve our own individualized successful way. There is not one absolute, every act just so, design. There is a uniqueness in teaching. Both in our own research and in the work of Dr. Kounin from Wayne State University it is clear that, within limits, there is freedom to develop this uniqueness. Yet there are parameters as at the point when strictness becomes meanness. At this point freedom for being individual ends. There is a pupil perception which defines the limit to individual freedom and uniqueness. Everything does not go. So, in addition to the fact that we learned there are many satisfactory ways to teach we must also learn there are also ways not to teach.

Another area of considerable discussion in our Conference was the matter of illness and problem behavior. Either there is illness, or there is no illness. There are disturbed children or just problem behaviors. I think this is one of the unattended agenda items. This rests eventually on what you believe is the "nature of human nature" and the "nature of human learning." There have been certain very different pronouncements these two days. It behooves us to test again and again our psychological beliefs. What you believe about the nature of human nature and the nature of learning will set the classroom design to which you aspire. There are renowned psychologists who take very different positions about this nature of human nature. Part of the argument as we were discussing and listening to each other pounding out agreements and disagreements echoed back to concepts about human nature. There are those who believe that the impulses of a negative nature which reside in the human organism have to be stemmed and blocked off. The major effort of socialization is to accomplish this. The impulse systems are seen as the enemies of society and those of us who would create social beings must deal with this internal enemy. Others believe that there isn't anything there but what has been learned and the goal is to replace unsatisfactory learning with new, desirable learning. Still others believe that within the human organism are native inclinations to seek health. The task is to release these inclinations so that they may more easily come to their own. This suggests a different theory about what we ought to do. If we take this position we anticipate certain self-healing. Deep down most children want to learn and they want to join the other individuals in reasonable behavior. They are like they are because something has prevented them from fulfilling their destiny, but within them resides the wish to be normal. Now if you take the first position, what is there ought to be stemmed, which is very unfortunate but that's the way we are built. If you think that you are just a bundle of learned responses, you create a new and different learning situation. If you believe you can release internal potentials for a change which reside in each of us, this suggests something different. I've found that we usually take the explanation that suits us at the time we are asked for an interpretation. But the matter of our phychological beliefs deserves a lot more clear thinking on the part of each one of us before we go on to method.

We focused quite a bit about another case of illness during these two days — particularly certain peoples' illness, namely teachers. We worry a lot about certain bad things that are going on in our field and bad teaching, in particular, gets most of the attention. We discussed how we might change these teachers. Perhaps this should be altered to the quest of how all of us could evolve into more useful professionals. Maybe we could do this by attending more to problem solving rather than roles or role exposition. This brings up the much discussed matter of teams, another interesting conflict. "We have a team and I'm in charge," is the way it usually runs. Maybe you read in Orwell's *The Animal Farm* that all animals are equal but pigs are more equal than other animals. In actuality this is the way most teams function: there is an ordained captain calling the plays. Again the dilemma of authority comes back to plague us. To some, authority denotes naked use of power which is a very bad thing. Because of our belief about the unhygienic nature of power we retreat from open examination of power and authority. We announce the co-equal teams that are about as unequal as you could design. There are many sources of inequality, some from role and some from ability to develop insight, some from differences in talent, some from training. Another inequality in the team is "I've been here longer than you have. You may be trained, but you don't know what this school is like I do." So all this talk about teams sometimes gets nauseous because it is more of a charade. We ought to be a little bit more frank about all of this. Behind lurks a concept about change: generating change forces the imposition of our values on others. We'd all like to influence other people to change as we think they should, but we wish it to happen by osmosis so that we wouldn't have to inflict our beliefs in an authoritarian way on others. This problem of power and teams deserves attention from all disciplines. We heard at least a hint of how to go about this. It was suggested we need joint discussions with the child that we are trying to help rather than for each one to talk to the child separately and then get together when he isn't there. Then we each try to put him together again from these second hand pieces. But we heard that it's possible to have multiple talks with the child. It need not be called therapy, counseling or interviewing. It is just a joint discussion of all those who are going to work together to help the child. So much for our problem of role authority. Openness and honest interplay between us would perhaps lead to some changes in our behavior. I would remind you that while we deal with sickness, we are ourselves not all sick. We have the capacity for change as normal people do through the use of insight, discussion and thought. It has become unholy to talk openly about someone else needing to change. Perhaps this is because we tend to be so afraid of change in ourselves. Data can help us change. Evidence—research evidence—can help. New ideas and concepts can lead to change. Confrontation can produce change. Obviously there is as yet no clear idea of where we're going and what therapeutic teaching is, or if we should even use such a term. In studies of the self concept of the teacher and other professionals, there is a lot of similarity. Possibly we could bring together the essential nature of several of the helping disciplines and have a different sort of a team. I'm reminded of one experiment where they tried to have team teaching but they couldn't do it because teams were very difficult to arrange. They needed the right "above" and "below" persons to work together although they still carried the euphemism of team teaching. It's very hard to have a co-equal team, and yet we learned that this work demands just that. I would say most of us can mature professionally by self insight, looking frankly at our behavior. We ought to do a little bit more of this and quit persisting in the little team which isn't there.

Another topic in this Conference was the goal of this special type of educational work. This will require considerable thought. We had some suggestions regarding the necessary professional characteristics needed and the mental health goals we are seeking. But just what is the description of the pupil personality we hope these people do achieve? This worries me because I don't know if I really appreciate what children will need to be like ten years from now to survive in the kind of society they're going to live in. So, while I'm trying to change them, I'm not sure I know just in what direction to aim. For example, how do I help a disturbed child, let alone a normal child, to acquire flexibility to anticipate preparing for a first job which he is going to lose because it will be outmoded and prepare for the six more they tell me he is going to have. He must still study for this job that he is going to hold for awhile before he's displaced by a machine to some other job if he is fortunate. How do I help him learn to live with little and big anxieties inside and outside because coming up looks like a period saturated with much anxiety. And most of them have too much already. How do we build in a capacity to cope with these anxieties which are going to plague us all in the decade to come? How do I get not the absence of, but controlled, aggression in children? This is something I don't know very much about. How do I help youngsters learn to sustain significant deep interpersonal relationships in a decade so devoted to making everybody's private life public? Still they must learn to cultivate intimate interpersonal relationships. Am I teaching him today's nonsense for tomorrow? How can I motivate an adolescent who understands that when tomorrow comes what he's learning today isn't going to be any good because it will be outmoded? How can I motivate our particular children to study for things that I don't even believe are going to be permanent? I close my eyes to change and what type of a healthy youngster I need to produce because I don't really know how to grapple with these issues. But it leaves an air of uncertainty. We are telling them how fast the rate of change will be and what we learn today is useless tomorrow and yet we say study. Study hard and learn. Learn this useless information that you won't need tomorrow and so you can forget it.

In closing I would say let us keep our humility in this heady situation of the next decade — all of us. The teacher who has successes and failures, the consultants who support, the philosophers who sensitize us and the psychologists who evaluate us and study our efforts.

On the way to the conference this morning with Dr. Cruickshank we were talking about the meeting and I told him a story about educational therapy — the most unusual I had ever heard. He said "You ought to end up with that." Right now I don't know how it connects, but I'm going to tell you the story anyway. I think it connects because this woman who was a vivacious, iconoclastic, different-type teacher had humility about her work and the zeal to do what she thought ought to be done, whatever it was. This is called "red wig therapy." I have pictures a teacher in Florida gave me which verify it. A child was entered in a special class. He was mute and diagnosed as schizophrenic. He refused to talk to anybody and he sat hunched up so that his neck almost disappeared as his head settled on his shoulders somehow. He wouldn't talk or communicate with anybody. After awhile, and it was about Christmas time, the youngsters were writing out paragraphs about what they wanted for Christmas. This was the first time he contributed and he wrote down he wanted hair, because he was bald. And he was absolutely bald. He wrote that he wanted hair for Christmas. He wouldn't, of course, *say* what he wanted because he wouldn't talk, but she read his statement and said humorously "I can't get you hair, but maybe I can get you a wig." You know, as you might say to a child. He had continually worn his hat in class to hide his bald head. Well, he became fixated on Christmas and this wig which he wanted so much and thought he was going to get. As the teacher told me, she had this thing going and she knew she had to get him a wig. So she began to explore wig getting, for which her professional courses had not prepared her very well. And she found out that if she went across the state she could get a wig for him, although the wig maker was distressed at the thought of designing a wig of false hair for a small child and also told her that it would cost $175, of which $25 had to be paid in advance and the rest when she picked up the wig. Now their therapeutic budget did not include money for wigs. There was no available petty cash. She went to a service club and I imagine that must have been quite a session when she said, "I want you to buy a wig for a kid for Christmas." As she said, "Me and my big mouth." I think it was really her big heart that got her involved, her sensitivity that got her involved, not her mouth; but anyway, she got the money. She went across the state and got the wig. It took quite awhile for the boy to get his head fitted, get the wig made and get it back. Then it didn't fit at all well. This was because he no longer kept his head stuffed into his shoulders. He stood tall and straight. So the wig was too large in the back. She said you could have put a clothespin over the extra part. He would have worn it anyway, he was that happy, but she took it back and she got it fixed. He was so proud of his new hair that his symptoms left him immediately and he began to converse. The picture of this happy youngster and that wig is some sight. It's a hideous wig, but it was beautiful to that child. He would not let it be washed or anything done to it if he could help it. He kept it on all the time. All the children were shown it. After about three months the teacher had a phone call from the mother. The mother said, "You must come to the house," and there was a tenor about her voice that scared the teacher out of her wits. She said, "I think I know what he's done. He's leaned over and dropped that thing in the john and flushed it down and there is $175 bucks worth of therapy down the drain." She was afraid to ask the mother but she went out. When she got there, he was there with his red wig, so her fears were wrong. The mother put the child under light and lifted the wig. There was a crop of short, fuzzy hair under his wig. No one had ever been certain, according to the history, why he had lost his hair in the first place. But he had. And now nobody knows why he got hair but he did. Even after peeking again to make certain, it was hard to believe for a long time.

In the last picture she showed me, here was this boy with a fine thatch of his own red hair. No more wig.

Well, I would say I think a lot of our business boils down to knowing where the child is hurting. What is bothering him? Have we the sensitivity in our interactions to find it? Those who interact with children are sensitive to their needs and they'll go about doing the things that the child needs in ways that we've never called therapy before, I think. I would suggest we not wait until research proves that wigs on a bald-headed little boy are therapeutic but to go ahead with the wig when you see the child needs it. Doing what your deepest human concern suggests seems to me to be one of the testaments that has come out of our two days of intense meetings.